D0470588

ATLAS of HISTORY'S GREATEST

DISASTERS
& MISTAKES

THE 50 MOST SIGNIFICANT MOMENTS EXPLORED IN WORDS AND MAPS

ATLAS OF HISTORY'S GREATEST

DISASTERS
& MISTAKES

THE 50 MOST SIGNIFICANT MOMENTS EXPLORED IN WORDS AND MAPS

Tim Cooke

METRO BOOKS
New York

METRO BOOKS
New York

An Imprint of Sterling Publishing
387 Park Avenue South
New York, NY 10016

METRO BOOKS and the distinctive Metro Books logo are trademarks of Sterling Publishing Co., Inc.

© 2013 by Quantum Publishing Ltd
Illustrations and maps © 2013 by Quantum Publishing Ltd

This 2013 edition published by Metro Books by arrangement with Quantum Books.

All rights reserved. No part of this publication may be reproduced, stored in a retrieval system, or transmitted, in any form or by any means, electronic, mechanical, photocopying, recording, or otherwise, without prior written permission from the publisher.

Publisher: Sarah Bloxham
Managing Editor: Samantha Warrington
Project Editor: Marilyn Inglis
Assistant Editor: Jo Morley
Copy Editor: Joe Fullman
Editorial Intern: Rebecca Cave
Production Manager: Rohana Yusof
Design: Andrew Easton, www.ummagummacreative.co.uk
Cartographer: Red Lion Mapping

ISBN 978-1-4351-4188-9

For information about custom editions, special sales, and premium and corporate purchases, please contact Sterling Special Sales at 800-805-5489 or specialsales@sterlingpublishing.com.

Manufactured in Hong Kong
2 4 6 8 10 9 7 5 3 1
www.sterlingpublishing.com

Contents

Introduction

MURPHY'S LAW FAMOUSLY STATES THAT WHATEVER CAN GO WRONG WILL GO WRONG. THIS MAXIM IS BORNE OUT WHEN IT COMES TO HISTORY—MANY OF THE DISASTERS AND MISTAKES OF THE PAST HAVE HAD AN IMPACT ON THE PRESENT AND THE FUTURE.

The true course of history is a long way from the version most of us learned at school, in which a succession of bold leaders or visionaries oversaw a steady stream toward progress and achievement. Accidents, coincidences, twists of fate: they have shaped the past as much as some kind of "grand design" that ensures each generation somehow improves on those that went before.

These false starts have often been caused by mistakes or disasters. The two are closely related, and they both have unfortunate consequences. In broad terms, a mistake is something that could have been avoided. Someone or some organization has to have made a mistake, whether consciously or unconsciously. Ultimately, there is someone to blame. A disaster, on the other hand, tends to be something unavoidable, something that happens to people, usually large numbers of people, without any conscious agent. The most clear-cut examples are natural disasters such as the Indian Ocean tsunami, Hurricane Katrina, or the eruptions that destroyed ancient Pompeii.

Even such a broad distinction is only of limited use, however. For one thing, many historical events have been examples of both mistake and disaster. Christopher Columbus' decision to sail west to Asia in 1492 was a mistake based on a false understanding of the size of the world. But his discovery of the New World— though these days often celebrated as a great achievement—was a disaster for the original peoples of the Americas, whose numbers were decimated by European diseases such as smallpox, to which they had no natural immunity. In the same way, Napoleon's mistaken decision to march on Moscow eventually cost the lives of some tens of thousands of his *Grand Armée*, for whom it must surely count as a disaster. When Adolf Hitler—a scholar of history, but apparently not of its mistakes— invaded eastern Europe, it spelled disaster for millions of people in Russia, Belorussia, and Ukraine, and ultimately the defeat of Germany itself and the division of Europe.

In contrast, some mistakes have only personal consequences, such as Henry Hudson's decision to spend the long winter with his ship stuck in the ice in an inlet of Hudson Bay in Canada. With the thaw, his unruly crew mutinied, put him and his young son in a small boat, and cast them adrift, never to be seen again. Lady Jane Grey, likewise, perished as the result of a mistake, but this time not her own, but that of the English aristocrats who intrigued to put her on the English throne.

Sometimes mistakes turn out not to have disastrous consequences. When King John I of England signed the Magna Carta, diluting the power of the monarchy, it was an error on a personal level. It failed to buy off for long the barons who were warring against his power (John himself would die within a few short months); but in the grand scheme of things, John's diplomatic misstep proved to be an early milestone in the development of Britain's democratic constitutional monarchy.

This book analyzes 50 of history's outstanding mistakes and disasters.

It describes what caused them, what happened, and what the consequences were. It ranges in time from ancient Egypt to the dot.com world of today, with stories from all over the world. But history is so full of possible examples that no book like this can claim to be exhaustive. Everyone will have their own candidates that they feel would justify inclusion—and they'd probably be right. This collection combines some well-known and highly significant episodes with less familiar calamities, such as the naval disaster caused by the magnificently named Admiral Sir Cloudesley Shovell, who did far more damage to the British Royal Navy than its enemies usually managed.

Everyone has heard the observation that those who do not know the mistakes of history are condemned to repeat them. But even from these 50 accounts that only scratch the surface of history's rich supply of howlers, it is clear that there are so many mistakes that one might despair of ever learning anything. When it comes to history, the best approach is sometimes not to question "Where did we go wrong?" but instead to marvel instead that we ever managed to get anything right.

Ancient World

The ancient world was littered with disasters and mistakes—pyramids constructed on shifting sand, new religions devised and defeated, and leaders who failed to recognize their own frailty. Croesus and Julius Caesar were the authors of their own misfortune, while the ruin of Pompeii was the result of natural disaster. The Fall of Rome, however, can only be blamed on a catalog of human mistakes.

The Failed Pyramid

EGYPT'S GREAT PYRAMIDS ARE JUSTLY RENOWNED, BOTH FOR THEIR SPECTACULAR APPEARANCE AND FOR THE REMARKABLE ENGINEERING THAT LIES BEHIND THEIR CONSTRUCTION. BUT EVEN THE EGYPTIANS' CELEBRATED BUILDERS DID NOT MASTER THEIR SKILLS WITHOUT SOME MISHAPS ALONG THE WAY.

Pyramid building started in Egypt in approximately 3000 BC, when the Third Dynasty pharaoh Djoser built himself a step pyramid, and the tradition would continue for 2,700 years. The remarkable structures were intended to act as funerary edifices for pharaohs and other dignitaries. Each pyramid and its adjacent architectural complex was the focus of many rituals, which had to be performed to ensure the pharaoh attained eternal life.

A pyramid's shape was crucial. Experts now believe that the four-sided, pointed shape was meant to copy the *benben*, a pyramid-shaped stone found in the earliest Egyptian temples, which was believed to symbolize the primeval mound from which life had been created. The Egyptians believed that the sun god Re emerged from the *benben*.

Sneferu decided to abandon the step-pyramid model altogether. He wanted his new edifice to be smooth-sided ... and bigger than anything that had gone before.

FROM STEP TO SMOOTH

The earliest pyramids, such as Djoser's, were built using a stepped technique. This was not unique to Egypt. In later millennia, the Maya, the Toltecs, and the Aztecs built step pyramids in Mexico and Central America. It was no coincidence. In order to attain height with ancient construction techniques, a step pyramid was the most obvious structure to use, rising from a base in layers that got smaller as they went up. But a smooth-sided pyramid was immensely more difficult to achieve, as the Egyptians would discover.

The pharaoh Sneferu (2613–2589 BC), is believed to have commissioned and overseen the construction (or partial construction) of three pyramids in his lifetime. The first was at Meidum and was

The second (or Bent) pyramid built by Sneferu, ran into instability problems during construction resulting in changes to the design.

probably started by his predecessor, the pharaoh Huni, who created a pyramid with seven steps. Sneferu filled in the steps to create a smooth-sided pyramid. During the New Kingdom, more than a thousand years later, this filled-in casing collapsed, exposing the steps, leading to the structure being dubbed the "Fake Pyramid."

SMOOTH-SIDED DISASTER

For his second pyramid (sometimes called the Bent pyramid), in the royal necropolis at Dahshur, Sneferu decided to abandon the step-pyramid model altogether. He wanted his new edifice to be smooth-sided from the start, and to be bigger than anything that had gone before. Its base measured 515 ft (157 m) on each side. It originally rose at an angle of 60 degrees, which would have given it an apex 405 ft (123.5 m) above the ground. This would have resulted in a pyramid with a volume three times greater than any pyramid yet built.

SINKING IN THE SAND

The square base was marked out by four shallow trenches, where quarried blocks of stone sat on a foundation of plaster and sand. The technique had been used successfully with the step pyramids, but once construction of the new building began, problems occurred almost immediately. The site was on the edge of an ancient riverbed, with strata made up of brittle limestone, shale, and sand, which soon proved unstable. As the weight of the pyramid grew, the foundations began to compress and move. Very soon, the baselines were wobbling under the weight, while the stone blocks used to build the interior corridors and rooms at the bottom of the pyramid started to twist out of alignment. As the workers placed more than 1.5 million tons of huge limestone blocks on top of each other, the structure started to sink—and the settlement quickened as the building grew. It was becoming clear that the builders' engineering skills and technological knowledge did not match their aspirations.

While the construction continued, the masons tried slight alterations to stabilize the mass. They changed the way they finished the stone, swapping roughly hewn blocks for smoother ones, which they began to set more accurately and lay horizontally to try to reduce the pressure. They kiln-dried the mortar that held the blocks in place. Still cracks appeared as the stonework shifted. The builders sank a small shaft in the center of the structure, known as the "Chimney," to hang a plumb line to try to work out how much it was moving. But they could no longer find the center of the pyramid and the masons no longer knew where to place the blocks.

BACK TO THE DRAWING BOARD

The solution—after work on the pyramid had gone on for some 30 years and with three quarters of its stone already laid—was to leave it unfinished. Sneferu started a new project close by. This new venture, requiring the largest pyramid workforce ever assembled, took 11 years to build, and eventually became the first true pyramid, known as the "Red Pyramid" because of the color of its stone.

RESOLVING THE PROBLEM

The successful completion of the Red pyramid—the third-largest ever constructed in ancient Egypt—showed the engineers how to resolve the problems of the Bent pyramid, and so they went back to complete it. First, they built a massive buttress around the original pyramid that was 50 ft (15.7 m) thick and at a shallower angle than the original. Laying the blocks more precisely than before, they built on top of this new wall a smaller pyramid of around 155 ft (47 m), sloping at an angle of just 45 degrees and giving the pyramid its unique "bent" shape. It is perhaps ironic that this monument to poor construction has survived into the modern era in a much better state than many other pyramids whose construction phase was less filled with error.

The map shows how the pyramids of the Old Kingdom are scattered along the length of the Nile. Sneferu would eventually succeed at Dahshur with the construction of the Red pyramid and go back to repair the Bent pyramid.

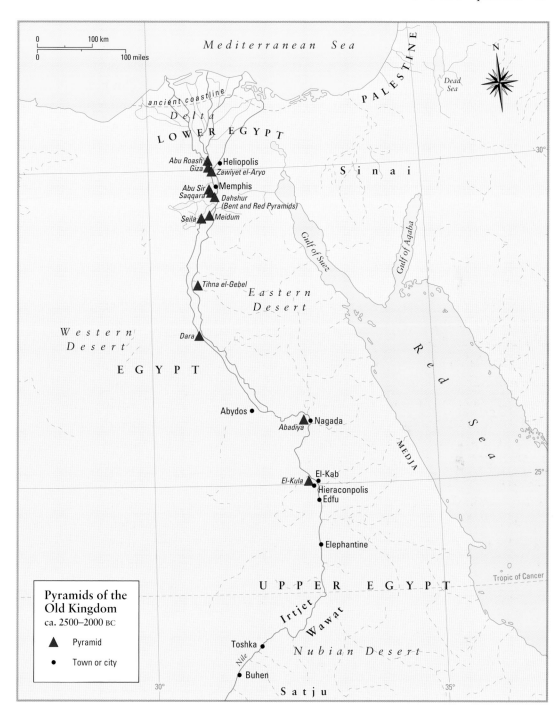

Pyramids of the Old Kingdom
ca. 2500–2000 BC

▲ Pyramid

● Town or city

A New Religion

THE EGYPTIAN PHARAOH WAS ALL-POWERFUL, BUT AMENHOTEP IV MISCALCULATED WITH HIS AMBITIONS TO MODERNIZE HIS KINGDOM. THE REFORMS AND NEW RELIGION HE INTRODUCED WERE INTENDED TO SWEEP AWAY ANCIENT SUPERSTITIONS; INSTEAD, THESE WERE QUICKLY SWEPT AWAY AFTER HIS DEATH AND THE KING'S NAME WAS ALL BUT ERASED FROM HISTORY.

By the time Amenhotep IV became pharaoh of ancient Egypt in about 1353 BC, the Egyptian state had flourished in the valley of the Nile for some 1,700 years. The new pharaoh was the tenth ruler of the Eighteenth Dynasty, which ruled the country for around 250 years during the New Kingdom. Experts traditionally divide ancient Egyptian history into three "kingdoms," when the state was relatively stable and united: the Old Kingdom (2575–2134 BC); the Middle Kingdom (2040–1640 BC); and the New Kingdom (1550–1070 BC). These were divided by three shorter and more politically turbulent "intermediate phases" when the state fell apart into smaller, warring states or came under the rule of foreign invaders.

> *A pantheon of gods was worshipped throughout the whole state, regardless of the temporary rise and fall in importance of other local gods.*

A CONSERVATIVE CULTURE

Throughout Egyptian history, different centers in the Nile Valley had been used as the capital under a succession of ruling dynasties. However, elements had emerged to provide cultural stability to Egyptian society. These elements included the importance of the pharaoh as the divine link between Egyptians and their gods; the use of hieroglyphs for ritual writing; and the rise of a cult of death in which the preparation of the dead for the afterlife became highly ritualistic. A pantheon of gods was worshipped throughout the whole state, regardless of the temporary rise and fall in importance

A map of the New Kingdom in ancient Egypt, during which Amenhotep changed his name and erected a new capital city at Akhetaton.

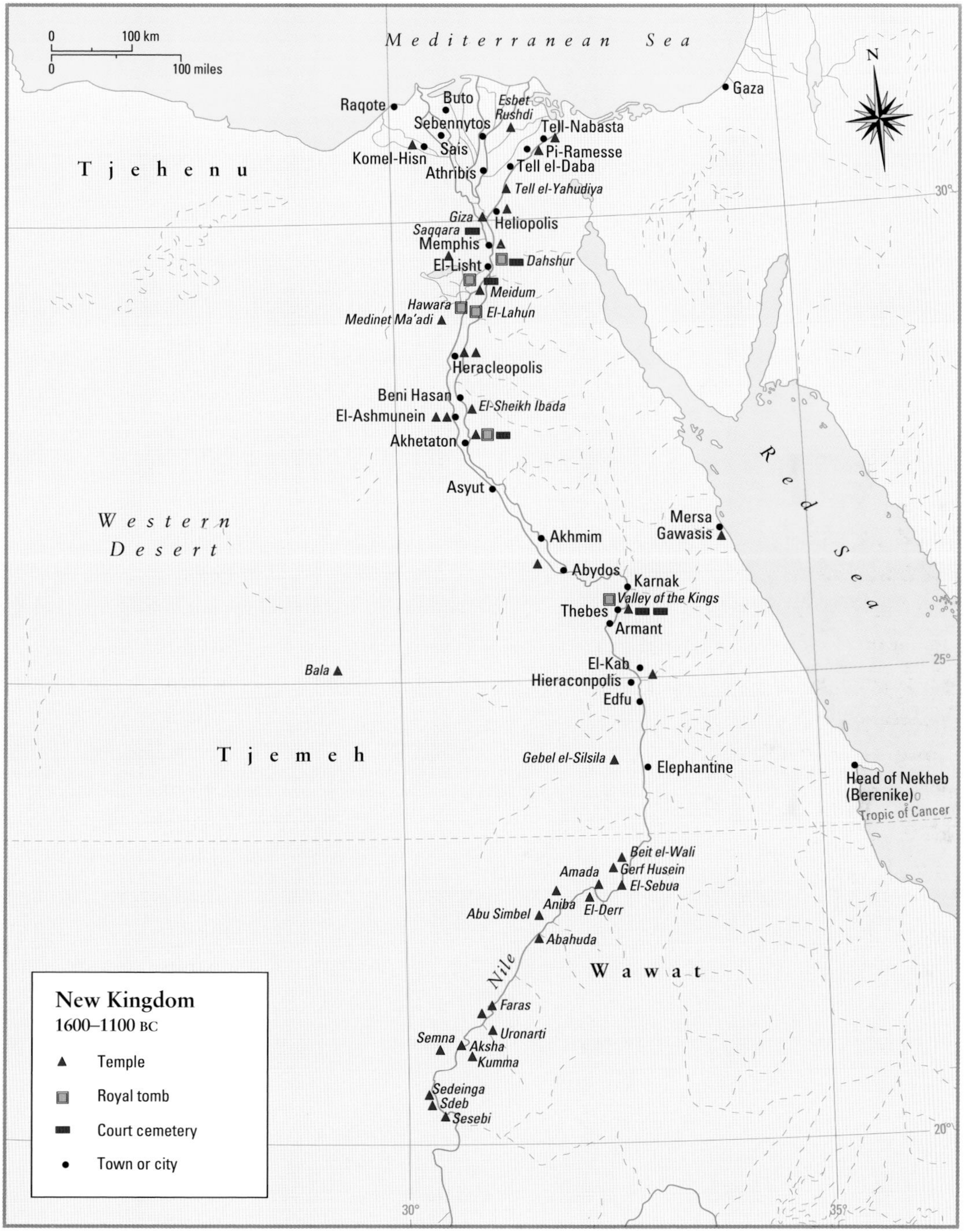

M e d i t e r r a n e a n   S e a

0 ___ 100 km
0 ___ 100 miles

N

Gaza

Raqote

Buto
Sebennytos
Sais
Komel-Hisn
Athribis

Esbet Rushdi
Tell-Nabasta
Pi-Ramesse
Tell el-Daba
Tell el-Yahudiya

T j e h e n u

30°

Giza
Heliopolis
Saqqara
Memphis
El-Lisht
Dahshur
Meidum
Hawara   *El-Lahun*
Medinet Ma'adi

Heracleopolis

Beni Hasan
El-Ashmunein   *El-Sheikh Ibada*

Akhetaton

Asyut

W e s t e r n
D e s e r t

Akhmim

Mersa Gawasis

R e d   S e a

Abydos
Karnak
Valley of the Kings
Thebes
Armant

Bala

El-Kab
Hieraconpolis
Edfu

25°

T j e m e h

Gebel el-Silsila   Elephantine

Head of Nekheb
(Berenike)
Tropic of Cancer

Beit el-Wali
Gerf Husein
Amada   *El-Sebua*
Aniba   *El-Derr*
Abu Simbel
Abahuda

W a w a t

Nile

Faras

Semna   *Uronarti*
Aksha
Kumma

Sedeinga
Sdeb
Sesebi

New Kingdom
1600–1100 BC

▲ Temple

▣ Royal tomb

▬ Court cemetery

● Town or city

30°

35°

20°

of other local gods. While gods such as Amun-Re and Osiris were important everywhere, others, such as the cat goddess Bastet, were mainly worshipped in a particular place—in her case at Bubastis where millions of cats were mummified.

Conservatism in Egyptian society was matched by strict artistic conventions. Humans were portrayed in set proportions

Within a short time of his death, Akhenaton's new capital was abandoned to the desert sands and his name erased from monuments and official lists.

and as physically perfect. Even in profile, people were always portrayed as having two eyes on the same side of their face. This did not reflect a lack of skill on the part of the artists; it was a deliberate gesture to show that the person being portrayed had two eyes and was not physically impaired.

NEW NAME, NEW RELIGION, NEW CAPITAL
Amenhotep arrived in this traditional, conservative culture like a whirlwind. No one knows why, but the new pharaoh was determined that things should change. He began with himself. Only five years into his reign, he changed his name. This was a significant gesture, because the names of the pharaohs had great symbolic importance, as they linked the kings with the gods. The king's new name, Akhenaton, linked the king with the sun-god Aton. However, in order to avoid conflict with the priests of Amun-Re, the principal deity, Akhenaton was originally content to treat Aton as another aspect of that god. As time went on, however, he increasingly argued that Aton was the only god—and Akhenaton was his only true priest. Akhenaton not only raised Aton above the other gods in importance, he had ambitions to ultimately do away with Egypt's complex pantheon of gods and goddesses altogether. He closed down the temples of other gods—diverting the income from their vast agricultural estates to the temples of Aton—and appeared to have tried to remove the names of other gods from monuments, although never with complete success.

Early in his reign, Amenhotep built temples to Aton at Karnak, center of the cult of Amun-Re. But then, to underline his devotion and break from traditions, he had a new capital city erected at Akhetaton, or "Horizon of the Aton," now known as el-Armana. The city was built in just four years, using mud brick painted with whitewash. Only the most important buildings—the Northern Palace, the Great Royal Palace, the Great Temple of Aton, and the Small Aton Temple—were faced in stone, but these temples were some of the most impressive in Egypt. They had no roofs, because the Aton was to be worshipped in the full light of the sun (delegates who came to visit Akhenaton from other parts of the country complained at having to stand in the heat of the day as they waited on the pharaoh).

Akhenaton even planned to start moving Egyptian tombs from the west side of the Nile, which the Egyptians identified with sunset, to the east so they would be associated with the sunrise.

The new religion and capital were not the pharaoh's only breaks with the past. He also undermined artistic conventions that had been in place for centuries. Instead of having himself and his wife Nefertiti portrayed in perfect proportion, Akhenaton had much more realistic paintings and sculptures made, which were unique for an Egyptian ruler. He appears with a sagging stomach, an elongated face, and "man breasts." As for his queen, she was noted for her (presumably genuine) beauty, as shown in a remarkable bust discovered in 1912; it is now on display in the Neues Museum in Berlin.

BACK TO THE PAST

Akhenaton died in either 1336 or 1334 BC. His new religion had somewhat less than two decades to become established, and it failed. Egyptians quickly turned their back on Aton. Akhetaton, built so quickly, was abandoned to the desert sands. In the second year of his reign, Akhenaton's son, Tutankhaten, underlined how completely his father's religious reforms had failed when he changed his name to that by which he would become known to posterity, Tutankhamen. Akhenaton's temples were destroyed, and their stones and sculptures used for other, more traditional building projects.

Furthermore, the names of Akhenaton and the four children who succeeded him were erased from monuments and from the official king lists. As far as Egyptians were aware, it was as if Akhenaton had never existed. It was only in the late nineteenth century that experts learnt of his existence and began to piece together the story of the monarch who defied centuries of tradition and ultimately paid the price by being written out of history.

Fall of Croesus

FAMED FOR HIS WEALTH, CROESUS WAS KING OF LYDIA IN ANATOLIA FROM 560 TO 547 BC. HIS DOWNFALL AND THAT OF HIS EMPIRE WAS THE RESULT OF HIS MISTAKEN INTERPRETATION OF AN AMBIGUOUS PREDICTION BY THE ORACLE AT DELPHI.

Croesus was born about 595 BC in the kingdom of Lydia in western Anatolia, in what is now Turkey, and inherited the throne at the age of about 25. Lydia was wealthy and Croesus was renowned as the first monarch to establish a system of coinage. From the silt of the river Pactolus, which ran through the Lydian capital at Sardis, he extracted electrum, an alloy of gold and silver, which he used to mint coins of a standard weight and value. Even in the ancient world, the king became legendary for his wealth; today, his reputation is reflected in the phrase "as rich as Croesus."

For all its wealth, Lydia was in an unfortunate geographical position. To its east was the mighty empire of Persia, ruled by the ambitious Cyrus the Great. To its west was ancient Greece and, on the Anatolian coast, the Ionian Greeks, who had settled there centuries earlier but were still closely allied to the Hellenic Greeks. Lydia was trapped between two of the most powerful empires of the ancient world.

Croesus' father had maintained a careful balance between the two great powers, but Croesus was more inclined to seek alliances with the Greeks to stop Persian power from increasing in Anatolia. But before he committed himself, he wanted to see if he had divine support.

Croesus sent test questions to Greece's major oracles—seers and priestesses who made predictions. Satisfied with the answers, he consulted the famous oracle at Delphi (there is a story that he also consulted an oracle at Thebes to be sure). This time he sent real questions: should he make war on the Persians, and should he make any formal alliances?

> *He decided to consult the famous oracle at Delphi...he sent his real questions: should he make war on the Persians and should he make any formal alliances?*

THE DELPHIC ORACLE

Since the eighth century BC, the sanctuary of the oracle at Delphi had been one of the most important shrines in the whole of Greece, drawing visitors from throughout the Hellenic world. The site was sacred to Apollo, because it was where the god was said to have killed a monster named Python, who guarded the navel of the earth. The oracle was a priestess of Apollo, called the Pythia, who passed on the advice of the god himself. Once a month—for only one day—the Pythia took up her position on a three-legged chair above a crack in the rocks of Mount Parnassus. She delivered the god's utterances in a state

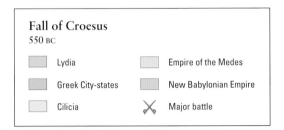

Fall of Croesus
550 BC

- Lydia
- Greek City-states
- Cilicia
- Empire of the Medes
- New Babylonian Empire
- ✗ Major battle

A political map of the Mediterranean region during the reign of Croesus shows the central position held by the Lydians.

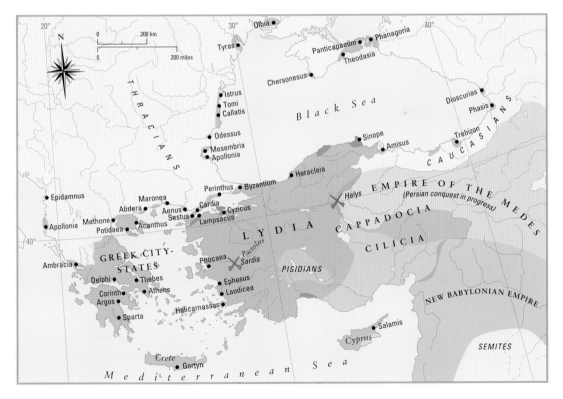

of delirium that modern scholars believe was probably the result of breathing the sulfurous fumes escaping from the crack. The Pythia's ravings were then interpreted by high priests of Apollo, who often gave famously ambiguous predictions to those seeking advice.

The oracle replied to Croesus' question by saying that if he went to war against Cyrus, he would destroy a mighty empire. She also told him to make an alliance with the most powerful people among the Greeks. To a further question from Croesus about whether his dynasty would last long, the oracle responded that it would survive until a mule became king of the Medes. To Croesus, that seemed a comfortingly long time.

WAR WITH PERSIA

Now Croesus acted; he made alliances with the war-like Greek Spartans, the Egyptians and the Babylonians. In 547 BC, Croesus besieged and captured the Persian city of Pteria in Cappadocia and took its citizens into slavery. Predictably, Cyrus now marched with his army against the Lydians. The two forces met near the river Halys in wintery conditions. There was no conclusive outcome, but the battle proved a strategic defeat for Croesus. Outnumbered, he withdrew to Sardis, leaving the Persians to claim Cappadocia for their growing Achaemenid empire.

Cyrus advanced into Lydia and met Croesus in battle outside Sardis at Thymbra. Croesus' forces outnumbered Cyrus by at least two to one, but the Persian's tactics were far superior. His archers and an improvised camel corps routed the Lydian forces. The Lydian survivors fled to the safety of Sardis, which surrendered after a 14-day siege. Lydia became part of the Persian empire, removing the last buffer between Persia and

FACT FILE
The Fall of Croesus

Monarch: Croesus, king of Lydia in Anatolia

Reign: 560–547 BC

Historic Feats: First monarch to establish a system of coinage; legendary wealth

Chain of Events: Croesus grossly misinterpreted a prediction made by the Oracle at Delphi; captured the Persian city of Pteria in Cappadocia in 547 BC; went to war with Persia; was taken prisoner and Lydia became part of the Persian empire in 547 BC

Outcome: Lydia was the last remaining buffer between Persia and Greece. When it became part of Persia, war between them became almost inevitable

Among the ruins at Delphi is the Tholos at the sanctuary of Athena Pronaia, a circular temple built between 380 and 360 BC. Located on the slopes of Mount Parnassus, the entire site of Delphi, which includes the famous Oracle among its many structures, is a World Heritage site.

Greece and making future war between the two great empires inevitable.

Croesus was taken prisoner. According to some accounts, he was treated well by Cyrus and became an advisor to the emperor; in others, he was burnt with his family on a pyre. Whatever Croesus' fate, it had become clear that the great empire he had been predicted to destroy was his own. His misinterpretation of the Delphic oracle's words has become a byword for reading one's own meanings into an ambiguous statement. As for the prediction about the mule becoming king of the Medes? Cyrus was the son of a Mede and a Persian, and so could be seen as a crossbreed ... like a mule, the offspring of a horse and a donkey.

Battle of Lake Trasimene

IN 217 BC, THE ROMAN ARMY MARCHED INTO ONE OF THE LARGEST AMBUSHES IN MILITARY HISTORY AT LAKE TRASIMENE. THE DEFEAT WAS A CALAMITY FOR ROME, BUT ITS FOE WAS NO ORDINARY SOLDIER . . .

The soldier in question was the great Carthaginian general Hannibal. The battle of Lake Trasimene formed part of the Second Punic War, a series of three clashes between the Romans and the people of Carthage. The first war, from 264–241 BC, left the Romans dominant in the western Mediterranean and Sicily. For nearly three centuries, Rome had built its influence through warfare in Italy, Gaul (France), and Greece. The Carthaginians were alarmed by Rome's power in Iberia (Spain), where Carthage had developed a significant commercial empire since its defeat in the First Punic War. Hannibal led his army in 219 BC to besiege and conquer a pro-Roman city there; and in spring 218 BC, he led his army across the Pyrenees and around the northern Mediterranean.

Hannibal reached the Alps in the fall—too late to cross the mountains, according to conventional wisdom. The Carthaginian had other ideas. Guided by allies from the Gallic tribes in northern Italy he crossed to Cisalpine Gaul (modern Piedmont) with some 28,000 men, 6,000 cavalry, and his famous war elephants. Hannibal's early arrival gave him the advantage of surprise, with the Romans still in their winter quarters. He defeated the cavalry of Publius Cornelius Scipio at the Battle of Ticinus, near what is now Pavia, driving the Romans south and swelling the numbers of his army with local Gauls.

The following month, in December 218 BC, Hannibal defeated an army commanded by Tiberius Sempronius Longus, who was provoked into attacking on a battlefield where the Carthaginian had prepared a trap. The Romans were massacred. Hannibal was now unchallenged in northern Italy.

The disaster caused alarm in Rome. Already the Senate had abandoned a plan to send an army to Africa to defeat

Carthage there. Now it elected two new war leaders to deal with Hannibal. Gnaeus Servilius Geminus took charge of Scipio's army, while what remained of Sempronius' own army—reinforced by two new legions—was to be commanded by Gaius Flaminius. However, the Senate had reservations about Flaminius. Almost his first action on being elected was to ignore the religious rituals that greeted a new consul and leave Rome to head north to join the army. The threat of Hannibal forced the angry Senate to allow Flaminius to have his own way, but it was right to be wary. He was as headstrong as Sempronius, but with more disastrous results.

HANNIBAL SETS A TRAP

Flaminius was on the back foot as soon as he reached his army. Heading south to protect Rome, he was overtaken by Hannibal and rushed to catch up with him, while Servilius headed to rendezvous with his fellow consul. Hannibal planned to provoke Flaminius in the same way he had Sempronius. He sent raiding parties into the countryside near Flaminius, and when the Roman refused to engage in battle, Hannibal simply marched around him into Etruria, cutting the legions off from Rome. Eventually, Flaminius had enough and, eager for action, he ignored his advisors' suggestions to wait for Servilius; instead, he led his full army in pursuit of Hannibal.

Hannibal found an ideal site for a trap, where the road passed through a narrow valley and across a small plain on the northern shore of Lake Trasimene (in what is now Umbria). He hid his forces in the wooded slopes that rose from the plain, where they could charge down on the enemy flank, and posted his cavalry where they could swing behind the Romans to block their retreat into the valley.

DRIVEN INTO THE LAKE

On the foggy morning of June 21, 217 BC, the overeager Flaminius hurried his column through the narrow valley onto the lake shore. The vanguard broke off to chase Carthaginian skirmishers—a ruse by Hannibal to split the Roman forces—and Hannibal gave the order to attack. At the sound of trumpets, Carthaginians and Gauls materialized from the woods and swept down on the Romans, giving them no time to draw up their famous battle formations. At the rear of the Roman column, Hannibal's cavalry drove the infantry into the lake, where many drowned. In the center, the Romans resisted for three hours against Gallic infantry, but were finally overcome. Only the Roman vanguard managed to break out of the trap, fighting their way to the east.

It had taken less than a morning for Hannibal to vanquish the might of Rome. Almost half the Roman army, some 15,000 men, lay dead on the field or drowned in the lake, including Flaminius, who had been cut down. Another 5,000 men were captured. Only 10,000 managed to limp back to Rome, carrying the alarming reports of the defeat.

In Rome, the news caused such panic that the Senate appointed an emergency dictator to face the threat. Quintus Fabius Maximus deliberately avoided battle with Hannibal in favor of skirmishes and raids, an approach now known as Fabian strategy. After Fabius' dictatorship, Hannibal won another resounding victory at the Battle of Cannae in 216 BC.

However, indecision prevented him from attacking Rome, and eventually the tide of war began to change both in Italy and in Africa, where the Romans finally launched their campaign. At the end of the Second Punic War in 201 BC, it would be Rome that emerged triumphant (while the third installment of the military trilogy would see Rome completely destroy Carthage). Still, Rome's defeat at Lake Trasimene would remain one of the greatest of all Roman military disasters.

The movements of the protagonists during the Second Punic War, and the sites of major battles.

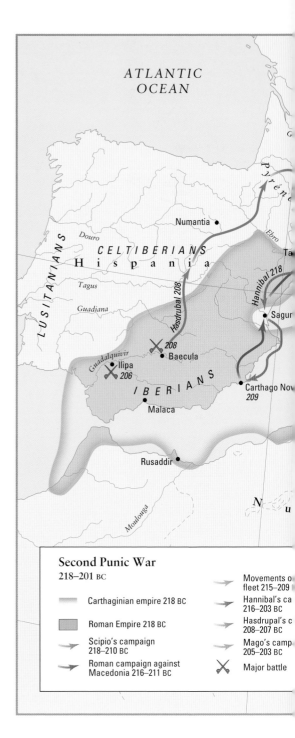

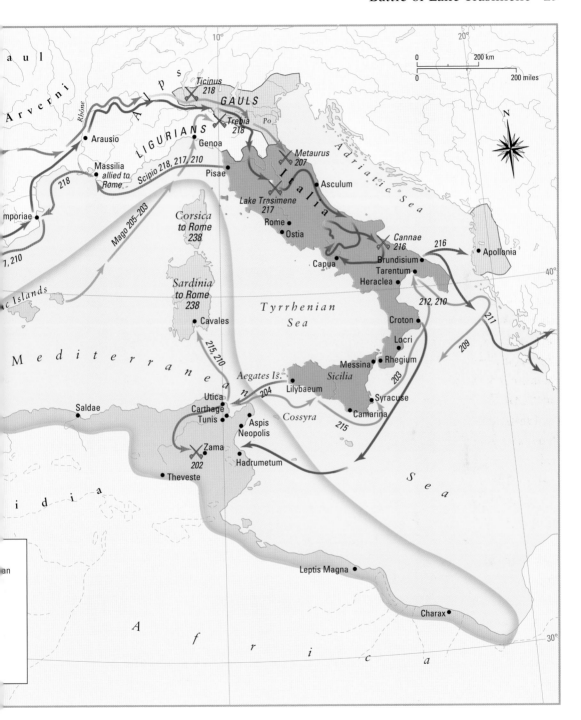

Gaul

Arverni

Arausio

Rhône

Alps

LIGURIANS

Genoa

Massilia
allied to
Rome

218

Scipio 218, 217, 210

Pisae

Ticinus
218

Trebia
218

GAULS

Po

Italia

Metaurus
207

Asculum

Lake Trasimene
217

Rome

Ostia

Adriatic Sea

Apollonia

Cannae
216

216

Mago 205–203

emporiae

7, 210

c Islands

Corsica
to Rome
238

Sardinia
to Rome
238

Cavales

Tyrrhenian
Sea

Capua

Brundisium

Tarentum

Heraclea

212, 210

211

Croton

Locri

209

Rhegium

Mediterranean

Saldae

215, 210

Aegates Is.

204

Utica

Carthage

Tunis

Aspis

Neopolis

Zama
202

Hadrumetum

Theveste

Messina

Sicilia

Lilybaeum

Cossyra

Camarina

215

Syracuse

203

Sea

i d i a

A   f   r   i   c   a

Leptis Magna

Charax

N

0   200 km

0   200 miles

10°

20°

40°

30°

The Ides of March

ON MARCH 15, 44 BC—THE IDES OF MARCH IN THE ROMAN CALENDAR—JULIUS CAESAR WAS ASSASSINATED BY A GROUP OF 60 CONSPIRATORS. CAESAR HAD BEEN WARNED OF THE PLOT BY A SEER, BUT TYPICALLY IGNORED THE WARNINGS.

Born into an old aristocratic family in 100 BC, Gaius Julius Caesar seemed destined for a minor political career typical for Romans of his social status. He made a socially advantageous marriage in 84 BC and set about making alliances with politicians, particularly those out of favor with the dictator Sulla. Caesar went abroad with the army to stay out of trouble, not returning to Rome until after Sulla's death in 78 BC, when his political career began in earnest.

THE TRIUMVIRATE

Upon his return, he became a military tribune, then *quaestor* (a financial official) in 69 BC, and by 59 BC, he formed a powerful triumvirate with fellow generals Pompey and Crassus. As his fortunes improved, however, he became an increasingly controversial figure. He was implicated in corrupt elections and had to rely on loans from his political allies to pay off his debts. That he was able to climb so

far so fast perhaps demonstrates the decline of Rome's political elite. In 59 BC, Caesar became governor of northern Italy and south-eastern Europe, and he set out to conquer Gaul in campaigns that forged his military reputation over the next decade. By the midway point of the century, the triumvirate was long dissolved—Crassus was dead and Pompey had become sole consul. He ordered Caesar to disband his army and return to Rome; Caesar refused.

CROSSING THE RUBICON

Julius Caesar marched on Rome to reclaim his power. In January 49 BC, he led his troops across a small river whose name has become synonymous with taking an irretrievable step: the Rubicon. Caesar's eventual victory in the civil war against Pompey and the nobles, which lasted until 45 BC, left him as Rome's dictator. He began a program of radical reforms, which included resolving the state's debt crisis, increasing the size of the Senate, strengthening the middle classes, and changing the Roman calendar.

Resentment of Caesar grew, particularly after his decision in February 44 BC to appoint himself dictator in perpetuity. According to the Greek writer Plutarch, a soothsayer warned the dictator that harm would befall him before the Ides of March. Consulting soothsayers was common practice among Rome's rulers.

On the Ides of March, Plutarch notes, Caesar met the same soothsayer while on his way to a Senate meeting at the Theater of Pompey. Caesar joked that he had reached the Ides safely. The seer reminded the dictator that the day had not yet passed. The omens were gathering. According to another ancient account, Caesar's wife Calpurnia had premonitions of disaster and was reluctant to allow Caesar to go to the Senate. It was Caesar's friend Brutus who convinced him to go, saying: "Are you a man to pay attention to a woman's dreams?"

SLAIN IN THE SENATE

However, Brutus was himself part of a plot that had been formed by senators, who included former friends, long-standing enemies, those with grievances against the dictator, and patriots alarmed by what they saw as the harm Caesar was doing to Rome. Ignoring a final warning from his deputy, Mark Antony, who had actually heard of the plot, Caesar approached the Theater of Pompey. The conspirators— who called themselves the "Liberators"— intercepted Caesar in front of a statue of Pompey in the portico.

According to Plutarch, Tilius Cimber stopped Caesar and grabbed his tunic while some 60 senators surrounded them. The senator Casca pulled out a dagger hidden in his toga and stabbed Caesar in the neck. Others joined in, stabbing Caesar as he fell, 23 times in all.

NO PLANS FOR THE FUTURE

The conspirators were so intent on getting rid of Caesar, they had not made any concrete plans for what would happen once the dictator was dead. Caesar had been popular with ordinary Roman citizens, who were outraged that an aristocratic clique had killed their ruler. Rome soon collapsed into civil war, with Mark Antony and Caesar's great-nephew and designated heir Octavian on one side, and the conspirators Brutus and Cassius on the other. The eventual triumph of Octavian's party led to the final end of the Roman Republic—a process begun by Caesar— and the creation of the Roman Empire, with Octavian (Julius Caesar's heir) taking the throne as the first Roman emperor as Emperor Augustus.

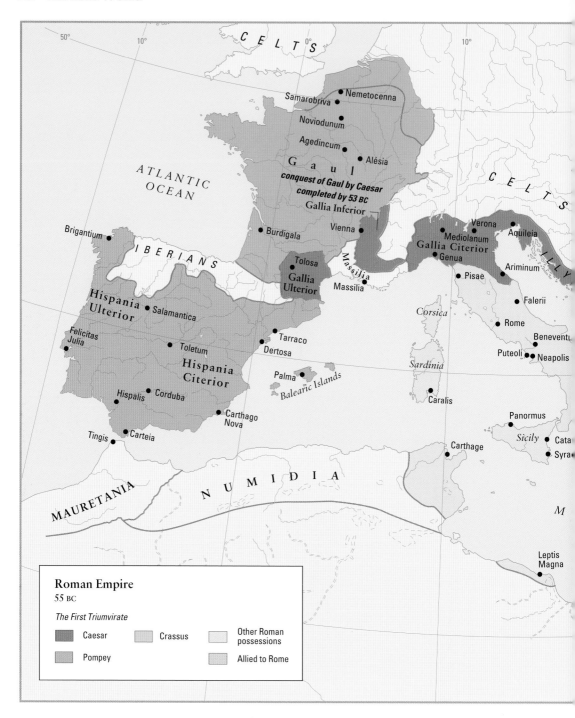

CELTS

Samarobriva • Nemetocenna
• Noviodunum
Agedincum •
• Alésia

ATLANTIC
OCEAN

G a u l
conquest of Gaul by Caesar
completed by 53 BC
Gallia Inferior

Vienna •

• Burdigala

CELTS

Verona •
Mediolanum •   Aquileia •
Gallia Citerior
• Genua
Ariminum •

ILLY

Brigantium •

I B E R I A N S

Hispania
Ulterior   • Salamantica

Felicitas
Julia •

Tolosa •
Gallia
Ulterior   Massilia •
Massilia

Corsica

• Pisae

• Falerii

• Rome

Beneventu

• Toletum

Hispania
Citerior

• Tarraco
Dertosa

Palma •
Balearic Islands

Sardinia

Puteoli • • Neapolis

Hispalis • Corduba

• Carthago
Nova

• Caralis

Panormus •

Tingis •   • Carteia

• Carthage

Sicily • Cata
• Syra

MAURETANIA   N U M I D I A

M

Leptis
Magna •

Roman Empire

55 BC

The First Triumvirate

■ Caesar	■ Crassus	□ Other Roman possessions
■ Pompey	▦	▨ Allied to Rome

Destruction of Pompeii

WHEN A COLUMN OF SMOKE APPEARED FROM THE TOP OF MOUNT VESUVIUS ON THE MORNING OF AUGUST 24, AD 79, FEW ROMANS LIVING NEAR THE COAST IN POMPEII AND HERCULANEUM TOOK MUCH NOTICE. AS EVERYONE NOW KNOWS, THAT WAS PRECISELY THE WRONG REACTION.

Some 30 miles (50 km) away, in Misenum, the renowned naturalist Pliny the Elder had eaten lunch after a bath and was relaxing. He observed the cloud, which his nephew Pliny the Younger, who was with his mother in Pompeii at the time, described 25 years later: "A cloud, from which mountain was uncertain, at this distance (but it was found afterwards to come from Mount Vesuvius), was ascending, the appearance of which I cannot give you a more exact description of than by likening it to that of a pine tree, for it shot up to a great height in the form of a very tall trunk, which spread itself out at the top into a sort of branches ... it appeared sometimes bright and sometimes dark and spotted, according as it was either more or less impregnated with earth and cinders. This phenomenon seemed to a man of such learning and research as my uncle, extraordinary and worth further looking into."

Pliny was one of Rome's most respected scientists, but he failed to connect the plume of smoke with a possible volcanic eruption, and his writings show little understanding of seismic activity in general. Earlier, in February AD 62, a severe earthquake had hit the region around Pompeii and Herculaneum, at the base of Vesuvius, which probably would have measured between 5 and 6 on the modern Richter scale. In Pompeii, many buildings were damaged and then collapsed. The city was

Pliny failed to connect the plume of smoke with a possible volcanic eruption, and his writings show little understanding of seismic activity in general.

The southern Italian peninsula and the island of Sicily remain areas of high seismic and volcanic activity due to their positions on the meeting point of the Eurasian and the African tectonic plates.

Pompeii
AD 79

● Volcano

ROME ●

S a m n i u m

L a t i u m

Sipontum ●

A d r i a t i c   S e a

Volternum ●

Beneventum ●

Neapolis ●
Herculaneum ●   ● Mount Vesuvius
Pr. Misenum
Bay of Naples   ● Pompeii   ● Salernum

A p u l i a

C a l a b r i a

Tarentum ●

L u c a n i a

T y r r h e n i a n
S e a

B r u t t i u m

Panormus ●

N

Mount Etna ●

Strait of Messina

S i c i l i a

Syracusae ●

0 _____ 50 km

0 _____ 50 miles

The ruins of Pompeii with Vesuvius in the background. Vesuvius is the only active volcano on the European mainland. The bustling Roman towns of Pompeii and Herculaneum were wiped out and covered with ash and lava from Vesuvius, and remained buried for 1700 years before archaeologists began to excavate the ruins in the eighteenth century.

still in the process of being rebuilt 17 years later, when the impending eruption of Vesuvius triggered a series of mini-earthquakes. The citizens of Pompeii were used to earth tremors, and indeed saw living in the shadow of the volcano in a favorable light. The volcanic land was highly fertile, covered with vineyards and small settlements.

THE ERUPTION BEGINS

On the morning of August 24, AD 79, a fine-grained ash started to fall around Vesuvius. Then, around 1:00 p.m., the volcano started to erupt violently. A huge cloud rose into the sky, thick with choking ash, pumice, and poisonous gases. Pliny the Elder, in his position as commander of the imperial navy at Misenum, ordered a boat to take him across the Bay of Naples in order to observe the eruption and rescue his relatives and others from Pompeii.

The town lay directly in the path of the ash cloud. The ash started to settle at 6 in (15 cm) an hour. A few people began to leave the town, but most stayed behind to wait out what they no doubt thought would be a passing storm. After a few hours, with the ash now 10 ft (3 m) thick, the wooden roofs of the buildings began to collapse, killing the people sheltering inside. Panic began to spread and more people rushed to leave. When the ash plume blotted out the sun and the sky turned completely black, the panic increased further. Pliny the Younger's mother became hysterical, but her son helped her to flee through the crowds of people screaming in terror. For another seven hours, the eruption continued unabated, and the ash continued to fall on Pompeii. Eventually, it became so thick that escape became virtually impossible for those left behind.

PYROCLASTIC DESTRUCTION

However, it was not the ash that killed the majority of people. About 12 hours after the eruption began, streams of volcanic material started to flow down the sides of the volcano's slopes. These red-hot pyroclastic flows—hot rock fragments, boiling gases and entrapped air—hurtled towards Pompeii at speeds of up to 60 miles (100 km) an hour. The first flow hit Herculaneum, a small town to the north of Pompeii, at around 1:00 a.m. on the morning of August 25.

Anyone who hadn't yet escaped was killed instantly. The first pyroclastic flow stopped just short of Pompeii, but the second one covered the town. People who had survived the earlier falls of pumice were now asphyxiated by the gases or burnt in the red-hot lava. By 8:00 a.m., further surges had covered much of the surrounding area. The landscape was devastated as far south as the Sorrentine peninsula and as far north as Misenum.

The number of victims was never precisely established, but probably numbered more than 10,000. They included Pliny the Elder, who died while trying to organize a naval evacuation of those fleeing the disaster. Many of the dead had sheltered in buildings that could not protect them from suffocation or the intense heat. Others died at the seashore, as they attempted to escape by sea. The two cities of Pompeii and Herculaneum were wiped out, buried beneath 13–16 ft (4–5 m) of ash and lava.

It would be a further 1,700 years before archaeologists began to excavate the ruins in 1748. What they and their successors found was remarkable: perfectly preserved streets, homes, and shops; tables still laid for meals with calcified grapes and bread; and dozens of holes left in the pumice by citizens cowering from the destruction. These holes were then filled with plaster to create molds of the bodies—and it is through their contorted shapes and faceless grimaces that we begin to truly comprehend the scale of the disaster on that summer's day.

Fall of Rome

THE PERIOD BETWEEN THE DECLINE AND FALL OF THE ROMAN EMPIRE AND THE
COMING OF THE RENAISSANCE NEARLY A THOUSAND YEARS LATER IS TRADITIONALLY
KNOWN AS THE "DARK AGES". ALTHOUGH MODERN HISTORIANS HAVE REVISED THEIR
OPINIONS OF THE ACHIEVEMENTS OF THIS TIME, THE EARLIER NAME SUMS UP WHAT
EARLIER EUROPEANS SAW AS THE DRASTIC CONSEQUENCES OF THE FALL OF ROME.

At its height in the first century AD, the Roman Empire stretched from the deserts of Libya to the lowlands of Scotland, and from the coast of Portugal to the mountains of Turkey. A combination of military might and trading power had brought a huge area, comprising parts of Europe, Africa, and Asia, and its peoples under the control of Rome.

Campaigns of conquest by Rome's legions had created the largest empire Europe had ever seen, unified by the Latin language ... and by public infrastructure.

IMPERIAL CONTROL
Campaigns of conquest by Rome's legions had created the largest empire Europe had ever seen, unified by the Latin language, by standard weights, measure, and coinage, and by public infrastructure that was a visible expression of the empire's power. That infrastructure found its most glorious expression in the buildings of Rome itself, but it was also echoed elsewhere: in the impressive barrier of Hadrian's Wall, built at the northern edge of the empire in Scotland; in the massive aqueduct at Segovia in Spain— 595 ft (181 m) long and 95 ft (29 m) high at its tallest; and in the harbor of Caesarea Maritima in Palestine. In towns all over Europe, private villas, public buildings, temples, and baths echoed those of Rome. The chief urban centers were linked by a famous network of roads, straight wherever possible, carefully drained and paved with cobblestones.

PAX ROMANUS
The construction of roads was a military imperative—the Romans needed to be

able to move their legions quickly to meet challenges to their power wherever these might break out—but the roads were also arteries of trade. Ease of movement, relaxed taxes and tariffs, a network of rest houses and the security from bandits and robbers offered by *Pax Romanus* ("Roman Peace") encouraged merchants to move goods freely throughout the empire and beyond, with imports arriving from east Asia via the Silk Road and from southern India via the dhows of the Indian Ocean.

This prosperity did not benefit everyone. As the empire grew, so too did internal tensions and external threats. Supply routes and food distribution were stretched over increasingly long distances. In large cities, such as Rome itself, it was sometimes difficult to keep the urban masses fed; the satirist Juvenal had already expressed the importance of "bread and circuses"—food and entertainmen—in keeping the populace happy in order to prevent them rising up and challenging the governing classes.

In far-flung parts of the empire, central government often had little authority, partly because of the time it took to get messages from Rome, and partly because local officials themselves were often very powerful. And around Rome's long borders hostile peoples—the Romans knew them all as "barbarians"—were waiting

to challenge the power of the empire. The Franks of what is now France, the Alamanni of Germany, the Visigoths of the Iberian peninsula, and the Sarmatians of Iran were among the various peoples to rise up against the empire.

AN EMPIRE DIVIDED

The man who took the decisive step to address the various issues threatening the empire stability was Diocletian, emperor from AD 284 to 305, who in 285 split the Roman empire into two linked halves, with the Eastern empire ruled by himself, and the Western empire, ruled by Maximian, a military officer he appointed to the post. The Eastern empire was already richer and more profitable than its counterpart, so when another military commander reunified the empire briefly in 324, he moved the capital from Rome to a new city in the east that he named after himself: Constantinople.

Constantine the Great, emperor from AD 306 to 337, founded his new capital on the site of what is now Istanbul in Turkey. The move laid the foundations for the permanent division of the empire in 395. But it also left the Western empire increasingly vulnerable. As the economic and political focus shifted east, and as various currents disturbed the internal coherence of the empire, so the crumbling unity of the once-mighty empire made it ripe for invasion. This already precarious situation was made worse when combined with a succession of weak emperors and a decline in military strength.

THE SACKING OF ROME

In 406, Germanic tribes—the Vandals, Alans, and Suevi—crossed the Rhine, Rome's traditional border, and devastated imperial territory. There were also revolts in Britain and Gaul. In 410, Visigoths led by Alaric I sacked Rome itself, an event that shocked the world. The early Christian writer St. Jerome wrote, "The city which had taken the whole world was itself taken." A second sack of Rome, this time by the Vandals, came in AD 455.

This slow and painful decline culminated on September 4, AD 476, when the Germanic chief Odoacer deposed the last Roman emperor Romulus Augustus. The empire in the west was finished, and with it much of the legacy of classical Rome would disappear (although in the east the Byzantine Empire survived in ever-diminishing form until 1453).

Within decades, the great cities became depopulated and their grand buildings fell into ruins; weeds growing among the cobblestones of the roads that stretched across thousands of miles of territory. The celebrated water systems, with their aqueducts and bathhouses, fell into disrepair. Bandits hounded travelers in the countryside, and the flourishing international trade that had underpinned *Pax Romanus* slowly ceased. Education declined, as did the speaking of Latin, so that soon there were few people who could read the inscriptions carved into the stone blocks they removed from Roman buildings to reuse elsewhere. Western Europe was slipping into what later generations would call, somewhat erroneously, the "Dark Ages."

The map shows the decline of the Roman empire from AD 400–450 and the advance of the once-conquered tribes across the empire.

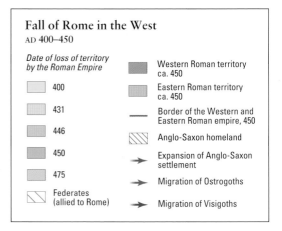

Fall of Rome in the West
AD 400–450

Date of loss of territory by the Roman Empire			
	400		Western Roman territory ca. 450
	431		Eastern Roman territory ca. 450
	446	—	Border of the Western and Eastern Roman empire, 450
	450		Anglo-Saxon homeland
	475	→	Expansion of Anglo-Saxon settlement
	Federates (allied to Rome)	→	Migration of Ostrogoths
		→	Migration of Visigoths

CELTIC PEOPLES

North
Sea

Baltic Sea

Eburacum

Angles

Saxons

TEUTONIC PEOPLES

50°

ANGLO-SAXONS

Londinium

ATLANTIC
OCEAN

Oesoriacum

FRANKS

Colonia Agrippina

Bagacum

Rotomagus

Mogontiacum

Lutecia

Remio

Augusta
Treverorum

EMPIRE OF THE HUNS

OSTROGOTHS

Argentorate

Turones

Augusta
Vindelicum

Lauriacum

Vindobona
Carnuntum

Cambodunum

Pictavi

Vesontio

Aventicum

Curia

Aquincum

OSTROGOTHS
from 454

Santones

Bituriges

Virunum

Pannonia

by 446, lost to the
Empire of the Huns

KINGDOM
OF THE
VISIGOTHS

Arverni

Lugdunum

Vienna

BURGUNDIANS

Aquileia

Emona

Mursa

Mediolanum

Verona

Siscia

Pannonia

Brigantium

Pollentia

Ravenna

Singidunum

Asturica

Legio

Tolosa

Genoa

Bracara

Arelate

Florentia

Ancona

Clunia

Salmantica

Caesarea
Augusta

Narbo

Massilia

Scodra

KINGDOM

Barcino

WESTERN ROMAN EMPIRE

Aleria

Rome

Barium

Dyrrhacium

OF THE

Tarraco

Olisipo

Toletum

Neapolis

SUEVES

Emerita Augusta

Corduba

Valentia

Tarentum

Nicopolis

Hispalis

Caralis

Codenra

Gades

Carthago
Nova

Rhegium

Panormus

EASTERN
ROMAN
EMPIRE

Tingis

Malaca

Caesarea

Hippo
Regius

Utica

Carthago

Messina

Syracuse

Mediterranean Sea

Sala

KINGDOM OF THE VANDALS

Sitifis

Constantina

Hadrumetum

Lambaesis

Theveste

Thaenae

Sabrata

Oea

Ptolemais

Leptis Magna

Berenice

30°

N

Boreum

Africa

0   200 km
0   200 miles

Middle Ages

The period that followed the demise of the Roman Empire, which earlier historians have called the "Dark Ages," was not devoid of cultural and intellectual endeavor. Nor, for that matter, did the Middle Ages escape the disasters and mistakes visited on earlier times. There were failed attempts at exploration and settlement, natural disasters in the form of the Black Death, and man-made disasters in the form of devastating fires. Disastrous battles, ill-conceived religious persecutions, and failed building projects were as plentiful in this period as in ancient times.

The Vikings in Greenland

WHEN THE VIKING ADVENTURER ERIK THE RED FOUND AN UNINHABITED COASTLINE IN AROUND 982, HE DECIDED TO COLONIZE IT. IN ORDER TO ATTRACT SETTLERS, HE GAVE IT THE MOST ENTICING NAME HE COULD THINK OF: GREENLAND. IT TURNED OUT TO BE ANYTHING BUT A RURAL PARADISE.

By the 980s, the Vikings of Scandinavia were feeling the pressure to expand. From their Danish, Swedish, and Norwegian homelands they embarked on a process of trading and raiding that would carry them as far as Britain and Normandy— named for the "Norsemen," or men from the North. They reached up along the rivers of eastern Europe as far as Russia and Turkey, to Iceland, and possibly even as far as North America (some archaeological evidence to substantiate this claim has been found on the eastern coast of Canada).

Viking sagas record that Gunnbjörn Ulfsson made the first sighting of Greenland when he was blown off course in the early tenth century, probably while sailing to Iceland from Norway. Other explorers arrived later in the century, but the most important was Erik the Red, who was filling in time during a three-year banishment from his Icelandic homeland for committing a murder. Claiming part of the south-west coast for himself, Erik returned to Iceland to persuade settlers to come and colonize his new land. One of the sagas reported: "He named the land Greenland, saying that people would be eager to go there if it had a good name." In 985 he set out for Greenland with 25 ships of settlers. Poor weather meant that only 14 ships arrived safely.

Claiming part of the south-west coast for himself, Erik returned to Iceland to persuade settlers to come and colonize his new land. He named the land Greenland.

The map shows Viking settlements in Greenland and possibly in North America from 985 to 1020, as well as the voyages taken by early Viking explorers.

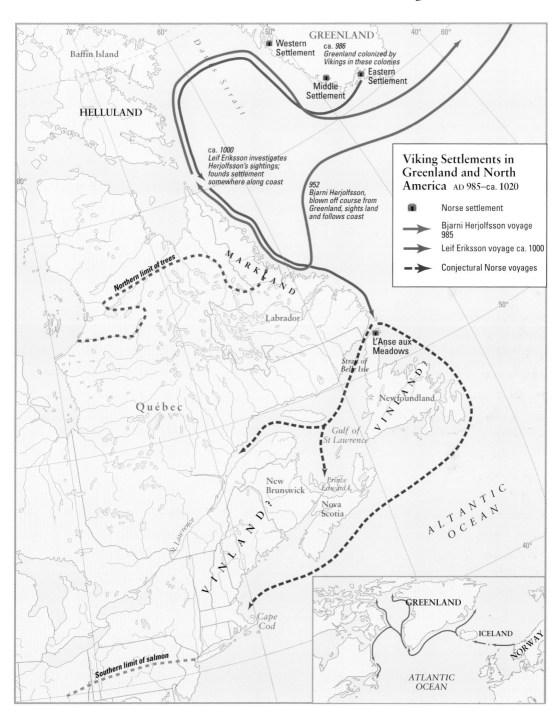

GREENLAND

Western
Settlement

ca. 986
Greenland colonized by
Vikings in these colonies

Baffin Island

Eastern
Settlement

HELLULAND

Middle
Settlement

ca. 1000
Leif Eriksson investigates
Herjolfsson's sightings;
founds settlement
somewhere along coast

952
Bjarni Herjolfsson,
blown off course from
Greenland, sights land
and follows coast

**Viking Settlements in
Greenland and North
America** AD 985–ca. 1020

Norse settlement

Bjarni Herjolfsson voyage
985

Leif Eriksson voyage ca. 1000

Conjectural Norse voyages

M A R K L A N D

Northern limit of trees

Labrador

L'Anse aux
Meadows

Strait of
Belle Isle

Newfoundland

Québec

V I N L A N D ?

Gulf of
St Lawrence

Prince
Edward I.

New
Brunswick

Nova
Scotia

A L T A N T I C
O C E A N

V I N L A N D ?

St. Lawrence

Cape
Cod

Southern limit of salmon

GREENLAND

ICELAND

NORWAY

ATLANTIC
OCEAN

The remains of a long-abandoned Viking church near Hvals close to present-day Qaqortoq in Greenland set in the austere landscape that would have greeted the first Viking settlers who came in the tenth century .

THREE COMMUNITIES

Greenland in the tenth century was not the snowy waste it is today. The medieval climate was at its warmest, and when the settlers sailed up the long fjords of the rugged south-west coast they would have seen grass and willow bushes growing on the slopes above the rocky cliffs, and extensive stands of birch woods up to 20 ft (6 m) tall. It was, indeed, a green land. What was more, the region was mostly unpopulated (there were Inuit peoples of the Late Dorset culture in the far north-west of the island, but the two groups did have contact for a long time).

The Vikings settled in three main communities: Eastern Settlement, with some 500 farms; Western Settlement, which had around 100; and Middle Settlement, with just 20 farms. In all, the population probably never reached above 10,000 and may have been as few as 2,000 (the current population of Greenland is 56,500). These hardy folk raised goats, sheep, and cattle, and traded meat, walrus ivory, and seals with Europe. However, the colonists were never entirely self-sufficient; they relied on Iceland and Norway for supplies of iron to make tools and wood for building boats. It was from Norway that Christianity eventually arrived in 1126, taking the place of the traditional pagan Norse gods.

THE COLD RETURNS

Life in Greenland was hard, despite first appearances. The grass was of poor quality and the soil was too thin to support extensive crops. In addition, from the moment the settlers arrived, they made conditions worse: they chopped down most of the birch woods for building materials and for fuel; their animals overgrazed the grasslands, loosening the soil and leaving it liable to erosion. Worse, a period of climate cooling started around 1300. Always subject to colder winters than the colonists' homelands, Greenland grew colder still.

As the summers became shorter and the dark winter spread through much of the year, the Greenland Norse virtually gave up on their attempts to grow crops. Instead they turned to pastoralism—rearing livestock—and to hunting. Over time, they kept fewer animals and relied more on hunting sea mammals, such as seals. By the middle of the 14th century, their diet was almost 80 percent reliant on food caught from the sea (it had previously been about 20 percent). In fact, their diet was so poor, they had to import food from far afield to supplement it.

ABANDONING THE SETTLEMENTS

Archaeologists and scientists disagree about the speed and the cause of the final collapse of the Viking settlements. Some believe the settlers effectively gave up and left to avoid starvation, partly because they had no tradition of the hunting techniques successfully used by Inuit peoples to get food in northern latitudes. Others argue that they simply moved on before crisis struck, either back to Iceland or to Vinland in North America (reached by Erik the Red's son Leif Eriksson, in about 1000). A further theory is that they were wiped out by Inuit or European attackers, although no evidence of a large-scale conflict has ever been found.

So desperate was the plight of settlers in Greenland that in 1345 the pope excused Catholics in Greenland from paying their tithes or taxes, an indication that the settlements were terribly poor. The Western Settlement was abandoned in around 1350. The last recorded visit to the Eastern Settlement came about 60 years later in 1406, when a ship was blown off course. A 1448 letter from the pope makes it clear that the Greenlanders had not had a bishop for more than 30 years. Shortly after, the Eastern Settlement seems to have also been abandoned. Erik the Red's colony had managed to destroy its own means of survival.

King John's Disaster

Magna Carta—the "great charter"—is famous as one of the founding documents of democracy in Britain. However, when King John signed it, he had no intention of abiding by its terms.

King John I was an uninspiring monarch. History has judged him harshly compared with his brother Richard the Lionheart, who became an English national hero despite spending just six months of his ten-year reign in the country (he complained about the English weather). John's modern reputation meanwhile rests on a failed attempt to overthrow his brother while Richard was away fighting the Third Crusade, his harsh taxes, disastrous military campaigns, and his unsuccessful (not to say entirely fictional) efforts to capture another folk hero, Robin Hood.

John became king on Richard's death in 1199 and was soon in trouble. He was forced to back down in a dispute with Rome after John tried to block the pope's appointee as Archbishop of Canterbury.

He also suffered at the hands of the French after he gave up his first wife and married a woman engaged to a French prince instead, resulting in the loss of Normandy (it was taken away by King Philip of France, John's feudal lord).

TAXING THE COUNTRY

However, John's major problems rested at home. In order to pay for the campaigns he mounted to reclaim Normandy, he introduced a series of unpopular taxes: he levied one-off taxes to pay for military campaigns, even when he was not campaigning; he taxed widows who intended to remain single; and he charged towns and markets fees to become established. More importantly, he imposed inheritance duties on castles and landed estates, sold

> *The result was that the very class of barons on whom John should have been able to rely for support became disenchanted with his ineffectual rule.*

the rights to offices, such as sheriffhoods, and imposed import and export duties, confiscating the property of those nobles who could not—or would not—pay. The result was that the very class of barons on whom John should have been able to rely on for support became disenchanted with his ineffectual rule.

Magna Carta, usually thought of as one document, exists in a number of versions scattered around the globe. There are versions in the British Library and the Bodleian in Oxford, with copies at several English cathedrals.

The situation grew worse as John filled the influential positions in his court with his own men—mainly minor nobles from the French desmene of Poitou—at the expense of the local barons, who he not only distrusted but threatened to ruin. No one, the message went out, could challenge the position of the king. Even those barons who were completely loyal to John were liable to fall foul of his suspicion and come under John's *malevontia*—royal ill will.

John further angered the barons by trying to force them to take part in military campaigns in Poitou, and in 1212 his nobles came close to launching a rebellion. Disaffection with the king was growing everywhere as he prepared yet another campaign against the French, even in the king's own household.

> *It also entitled free Englishmen to justice, protected them from being jailed without trial, and guaranteed the freedom of the Church.*

Feudal barons who had served John loyally, but who were often deeply in debt to him, were particularly discontent. The situation grew worse after the Battle of Bouvines against the French in 1214, where defeat for John meant the end of any chance of recapturing Normandy. It was his last campaign on French soil.

THE BARONS' REVOLT

By now, John was so unpopular with his subjects that in late spring 1215 some of the most powerful barons in the kingdom—mainly from the north and east—rebelled against him and marched on London. When they got to the capital, Londoners opened the city gates to let them in, so low was John's popularity there. The rebels called themselves "the Army of God," and if they had been united enough to agree on an alternative monarch, they might have gone on to overthrow John. As it was, however, they came to an agreement through the arbitration of the Archbishop of Canterbury Stephen Langton. On June 15, 1215, the king and some 62 barons met in a water meadow near the river Thames at Runnymede, some 20 miles (32 km) west of London. The barons had drawn up a document based on the provisions of the so-called Charter of Liberties, which had been granted by Henry I in 1100. The charter placed limits on the power of the king to raise taxes without the approval of a new committee—which would, of course, be made up of barons. It also entitled free Englishmen to justice, protected them from being jailed without trial, and guaranteed the freedom of the Church. In return for John signing the charter, the rebels would leave London and send their army home.

John stamped his seal on the document, but neither he nor the barons had any real intention of sticking to its provisions. The barons refused to leave London or disband their army, while John appealed to Pope Innocent III to reinforce his right to rule, which the pope duly did.

The outcome was the First Barons' War, which began well for John when he captured Rochester Castle and then headed up the country to attack the rebels in the north. But then John fell sick, possibly with dysentery, and somehow managed to lose the Crown Jewels in the sea while he was crossing a marshy inlet of the Wash in Lincolnshire. It is thought that the shock may have helped hasten the king's demise a few days later, on October 18, 1216.

John's death saved the document he had signed, now known as the Magna Carta. It became law under his son, Henry III in 1225 and was promulgated again some 50 years later. It remains the bedrock of English and Welsh law and of all constitutional monarchies, recognizing for the first time that the monarch only rules with the assent of the people. It set crucial limitations on the king's power and is recognized as a cornerstone of British democracy. However, if the men who had signed it had anything to do with it, Magna Carta probably would have vanished without much trace not long after it was created. John had thrown away the divine right of kings—it would never again be retrieved.

Ironically, something that was a mistake for the king turned out to be a boon for the country and for all consitutional monarchies since. It limited the powers of the king and meant that his will was not arbitrary, that the law of the land would prevail, and that he, too, was bound by the law. It has had a profound influence on the drafting of constitutions of many nations, including the American constitution.

FACT FILE

King John's Disaster

Monarch: King John I of England

Born: 24 December 1166

Died: 19 October 1216

Reign: 1199–1216

Chain of Events: John introduced unpopular taxes; filled the court with his own men; suffered a defeat at the Battle of Bouvines in 1214; barons rebelled in 1215; Magna Carta signed in 1215; the First Barons' War (1215–1217)

Legacy: John's death saved Magna Carta, which became law in 1225. It remains the foundation for English and Welsh law and for all constitutional monarchies

Leaning Tower of Pisa

IT WOULD BE FORGIVABLE TO IMAGINE THAT THE FAMOUS LEAN OF THE LEANING TOWER OF PISA WAS THE RESULT OF SETTLEMENT LONG AFTER CONSTRUCTION WAS FINISHED. IN FACT, THE LEAN WAS ALREADY APPARENT SOON AFTER THE MONUMENT WAS BEGUN, BUT THE PISANS DECIDED TO CARRY ON AND COMPLETE IT ANYWAY.

The Leaning Tower owes its existence to Pisan widow Berta de Bernardo, who in 1172 left "sixty coins" in her will for the construction of a freestanding campanile (bell tower) on a site in the city's cathedral square. Work on a cathedral had begun in 1064 and on a new baptistery in 1153. The splendor of the white marble buildings of what was later dubbed the Piazza dei Miracoli or the Square of Miracles, was intended to reflect and glorify the status of 12th-century Pisa. The city-state was, at that point in history, an important maritime power in western Europe and beyond. In 1111, it had concluded a treaty with Byzantium, allowing Pisan merchants free access to the Holy Land, which greatly enhanced the city's wealth and prestige.

> *The structure is less solid than it first appears, being a hollow masonry cylinder made from two concentric marble walls filled with mortar and rubble...*

THAT SINKING FEELING

Work started on the bell tower in 1173 but came to a halt five years later with just three stories completed. The tower was already shifting from the vertical. The unknown architect of the project had sited the campanile behind the cathedral, but the ground there was made up of clay, fine sand, and shells (the name "Pisa" actually comes from a Greek word meaning "marshy land"). As each new story was added, the tower sank farther into the soft ground.

The structure is less solid than it first appears, being a hollow masonry cylinder made from two concentric marble walls filled with mortar and rubble, with six

Pisa eventually became part of the republic of Florence, one of the leading powers in medieval and Renaissance Italy.

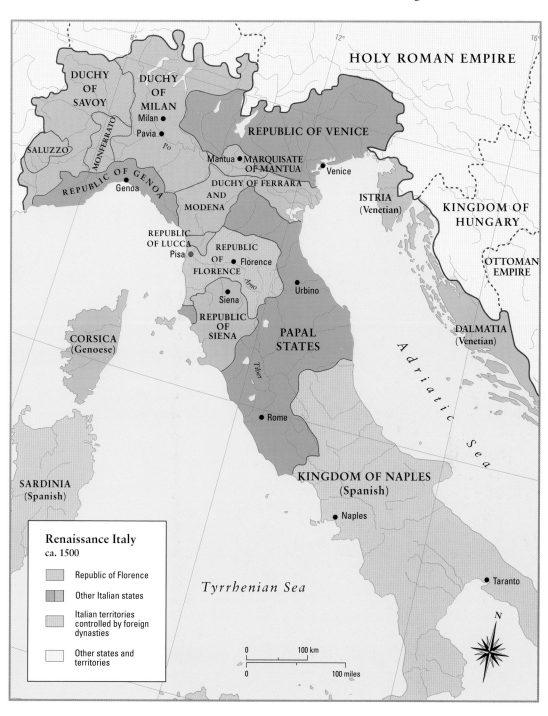

Renaissance Italy
ca. 1500

Republic of Florence

Other Italian states

Italian territories
controlled by foreign
dynasties

Other states and
territories

Leaning Tower of Pisa as it now stands. Work undetaken by Professor John Burland of Imperial College, London, has stabilized the tower and it is no longer moving.

of Pisa entering a series of wars to maintain its trading supremacy, or it may have been a deliberate effort to allow the tower to settle. The second phase of building began in 1272 under the architect Giovanni di Simone, who stuck to the original Romanesque design even though it was no longer fashionable. By 1278, Simone had reached the seventh cornice, at the top of the sixth loggia, building the upper floors with one side slightly higher than the other to try to compensate for the tilt. Still, by 1298, the tower was leaning enough to merit a commission to investigate the causes. This would be the first of many commissions over the next seven centuries to try to work out a solution to the problem.

THE SEARCH FOR STABILITY

By the time the tower was officially completed in 1370, it inclined 1.6 degrees from the vertical. Over the next few centuries, the sagging of the tower would

loggias (open galleries, supported by pillars) around the exterior and a bell chamber at the top. But the tower still weighs some 16,000 tons (14,500 tonnes) and needed far deeper foundations than the 10 ft (3 m) provided.

Once work was abandoned, it would not resume for almost 100 years. The long layoff may have been the result be mirrored by Pisa's general economic and political decline. Eventually, the city became a backwater of Tuscany. In 1817, two visiting English architects, Edward Cresy and George Ledwell Taylor, measured the tilt at the top of the tower as 12 ft 7 in (3.84 m) off the vertical. It was apparent that the tower would topple over if nothing was done. The next century and a half saw a series of ill-conceived attempts to correct the tilt, beginning with Alessandro della Gherardesca, who excavated a *catino* (walkway) around its base, only to discover that this allowed water to flood the tower's lower reaches and made its movement even worse. An earthquake in 1846 further destabilized the foundations.

After the campanile in Saint Mark's Square in Venice collapsed in 1902, another commission was set up to solve the problem of Pisa's tower. A flood of commissions followed, but no practical ideas were forthcoming until 1934, when an unlikely expert joined the debate. The Italian dictator, Benito Mussolini, saw the Leaning Tower as an unfit symbol of Italian prowess. He approved a plan to drill 361 holes into the base of the campanile and inject 90 tons (80 tonnes) of concrete into the cylinder to stabilize it. The outcome was nearly disastrous—the tower almost fell over.

Future efforts were no more successful and the risk of the structure falling grew so great that the campanile had to be closed to the public in 1990, shortly after the Civic Tower in Pavia had collapsed, killing four people. Another commission came up with yet more solutions, including using floating helium balloons to pull the tower straight and relandscaping the lawns around the tower so they sloped and gave the impression of the tower being upright. In 1992, an attempt to shore up the lower stories with steel tendons and lead counterweights led to an outcry at the unsightly appearance they created. Three years later, in what became known as Black September, an attempt to provide a more aesthetic solution by using ten underground steel anchors to hold the structure in place almost toppled the tower.

In 1998, Professor John Burland of Imperial College, London, finally came up with a solution. Over two years, small amounts of soil were extracted daily from the north side to allow gravity to coax the tower upright. At the end of the project, the tower still inclined by 13 ft (4 m) off the vertical at its top—but it will not move anymore. In 2003, a new drainage system was installed and the Leaning Tower of Pisa stopped moving entirely. Barring earthquakes, it is predicted to remain stable for the next 200 years.

The Black Death

IN JUST FOUR YEARS, AN EPIDEMIC KILLED SOME 25 MILLION PEOPLE IN EUROPE. IN ENGLAND ALONE, THE POPULATION FELL BY ALMOST A HALF. THE FABRIC OF SOCIETY WAS SHREDDED BY ONE OF THE WORST DISASTERS IN HISTORY: THE BLACK DEATH.

The first recorded outbreak of the disease in Europe came in the Crimea, at the Genoese Black Sea trading post Kaffa (modern Feodosiia), in 1347. The disease had most likely arrived in the Crimea from Asia, probably carried along the Silk Road route from eastern Asia by the Mongol soldiers of the Golden Horde. Indeed, a Mongol army was laying siege to the trading post when its soldiers unexpectedly started to die. The Mongols catapulted the rotting corpses into the trading post, hoping either to infect its defenders or that the foul smell would force them to surrender.

THE DISEASE SPREADS

When the Genoese fled back to Italy, the disease went with them. It arrived in the Mediterranean at Sicily in October 1347. The disease then began to spread through Europe, traveling, according to some accounts, at the rate of around 2½ miles (4 km) a day. Two distinct routes spread out from the Mediterranean port—one went through mainland Italy, Spain, and France, reaching England and Ireland by 1348; while another spread through Germany, Hungary, Austria, Switzerland, and the Low Countries in 1349, finally reaching Scandinavia and the Baltic countries by 1350. Meanwhile, the pandemic had also spread from the Black Sea to Egypt, and from there down the eastern coast of the Mediterranean and south into the Middle East.

The effect of the disease was uneven. Some regions were relatively lightly affected, while others lost as much as 80 percent of their populations. Milan and Flanders suffered only slightly, for example, while Tuscany and Catalonia were hit very hard. Towns tended to endure far higher fatality rates than rural areas because of the density of their populations. But overall, the highest incidents of the disease came among closed monastic communities. Rich and poor alike suffered, with some of the leading members of royal families and the nobility being struck down.

To make matters worse, no one really understood how the disease spread. The prevailing medical opinion was that it was caused by an evil fog or miasma, which meant that measures that might have slowed its spread, such as imposing quarantines, were not adopted. Modern scientists believe that the disease was most likely the bubonic plague—possibly combined with a form of pneumonic plague, which has higher mortality rates—caused by the *Yersinia pestis* bacterium, which is carried by fleas harbored on rats.

BUBOES, PUS, AND BLOOD

Whatever the precise nature of the disease, its progress was common. The first symptoms were the appearance of lumps—the buboes that gave the disease its name—in the victim's armpits and groin. These sores could be as large as apples, purplish, and often oozed pus and blood. Black spots spread over the body of the victim, who would begin to vomit blood and suffer a high fever. The bacterium also affected the victim's lungs, so they could no longer breathe, and poisoned their blood. Contemporary reports note that victims had foul breath, as if rotting from inside. Death came within seven days.

Lacking a medical explanation for the calamity, many Europeans saw it as a form of divine punishment for sins ranging from greed and heresy, to fornication and worldliness. They sought God's forgiveness in order to stop the plague. Others scourged themselves, flailing their bodies in public displays of their guilt and suffering. Some Christians turned from excess and lived modestly in small communities, consuming small amounts of the finest foods and wines. But others decided that the best way to react to the threat of imminent death was to indulge themselves, drinking and eating as much as they could, and even moving into homes left empty by victims of the plague.

Fires burnt across cities to try and stop the foul air from spreading. People carried flowers and scented herbs to hold to their noses, reasoning that the perfume would scent the air and prevent the disease from reaching them. Everyone avoided anyone who showed any signs of illness; families would abandon sick members and domestic servants ran off at the first sign of sickness in a household.

A SOCIETY TRANSFORMED

By 1352, the disease had passed, but it had left behind a society changed forever. The population had fallen so rapidly that there was a shortage of people available to work. According to one theory, the lack of manpower was responsible for the relative lack of warfare in the second half of the 14th century. Farms lay empty and marginal land was abandoned altogether. More importantly, the medieval feudal system that had bound peasants to their landowning barons began to fragment. Peasants found they could earn wages from new employers desperate for labor. Many left the estates where they had lived, and in doing so left their traditional duties of service and loyalty to their feudal lords. Wages rose dramatically, as did the cost of many goods (except food, which was in abundant supply for such a greatly reduced population). The Black Death signaled the transition of western Europe from a feudal to a cash-based economy.

The authority of the Catholic Church had been greatly undermined. None of the religious attempts to halt the plague had any effect. Meanwhile, Europe's minorities had suffered disproportionately. In their eager quest for scapegoats for the pandemic, Christians blamed so-called heretics, such as the Jews, and massacred almost 140,000; they are the often overlooked victims of the Black Death.

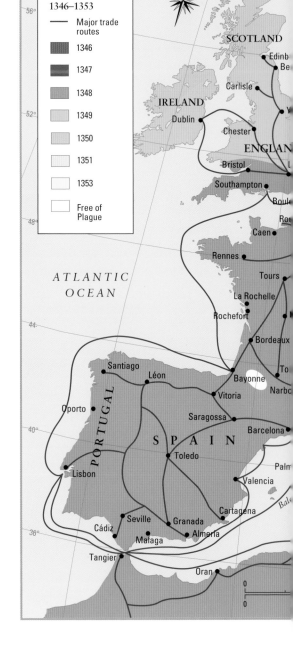

The Black Death seemed to spread along major trade routes: the map shows the spread of the disease from 1346 to 1353.

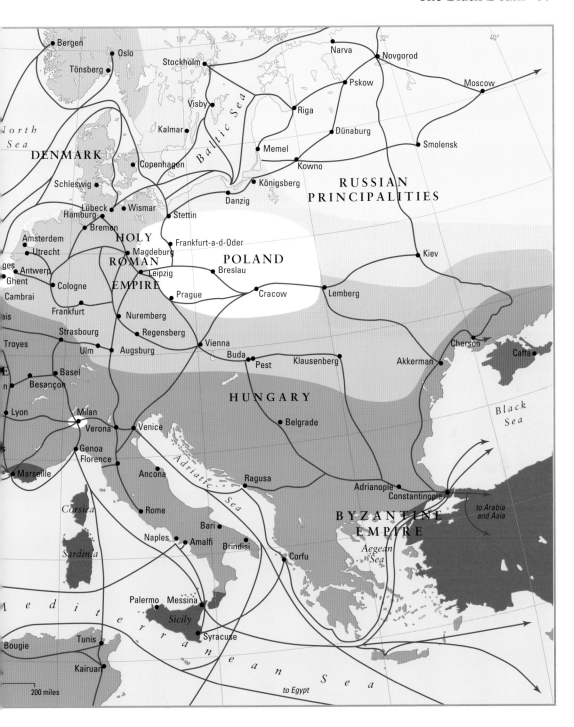

Peasants' Revolt

In 1381, a popular uprising in the south-east of England reflected huge shifts in the basis of society. The Great Revolt seemed to have some chance of winning concessions from the government of King Richard II, until its leaders made a disastrous miscalculation.

The roots of the Peasants' Revolt rest in the general spirit of uncertainty that gripped northern Europe in the late 14th century. The continent was still reeling from the Black Death, which had reduced the overall population by more than one third. With a lack of labor available for farming, some peasants broke from the serfdom that had held them to their lords, and sought to earn wages in a free market.

For many Englishmen, these officials were a byword for corruption and the figureheads of the new king's unpopular policies....

TRYING TO TURN BACK THE CLOCK

Alarmed landowners petitioned the king to help them. In 1351, King Edward III had introduced the Statute of Labourers to restore wages to pre-Black Death levels and punish peasants for seeking new work. This attempt to turn back the clock infuriated serfs who had begun to establish themselves as farmers or craftsmen. Chief among the hard-line landlords who were intent on enforcing the old system was the Catholic Church. Many peasants, or villeins, were in turn attracted to the preaching of groups, such as the Lollards, who railed against the corruption of the Church's clergy.

Edward III died in 1377 and was succeeded by his son Richard II, at the age of 10. Many observers quoted an ominous verse from the Bible: "Woe be to thee, O land, when thy king is a child." The new king's youth meant that his advisers exercised a great influence. They included John of Gaunt, Duke of Lancaster, and Simon of Sudbury, who was both Archbishop of Canterbury and Lord Chancellor. For many, these officials were a byword for corruption and the figureheads for the new king's unpopular policies.

An engraving showing William Walworth, the Lord Mayor of London, killing Wat Tyler at Smithfield in 1381.

Richard II not only failed to assuage his subjects' frustrations, he inflamed them further. In 1381, he imposed a poll tax to be paid by all adult males. This seemed to the English like an exercise in lining the pockets of the nobles. The new tax was widely regarded as unfair, allowing reductions for some payers but not for others, and too expensive. At one shilling, it was almost the average monthly wage for a man and his family.

UPRISINGS IN KENT AND ESSEX
In May 1381, a tax collector arrived at the village of Fobbing in Essex to collect the new levy. The local landowner drove him out of the village. When another official came to investigate, he was attacked by villagers in nearby Brentwood. The protest quickly became an uprising throughout Essex and the neighboring county of Kent.

Rebels captured Rochester and Canterbury in Kent and Colchester, Brentwood, and Chelmsford in Essex. They released prisoners, burnt any documents associated with serfdom, and forced the landlords to grant their villeins freedom. The rebels made everyone swear loyalty to "King Richard and the true Commons"—it was the king's advisers they blamed, not the king himself.

Within a month, more than 60,000 people had moved on London in an armed uprising. At their head was a man from Kent, Wat Tyler, of whose earlier life almost nothing is known. On the way, they were addressed by the Lollard priest John Ball, who preached social revolution: "If God had intended some to be serfs and others Lords, he would have made a distinction between them at the beginning." Ball asked his listeners a famous question: "When Adam delved and Eve span, who was then the gentleman?"

Tyler led his band across London Bridge into the heart of the realm. Meanwhile, the band from Essex also made their way into the capital. Led by Jack Straw, they attacked properties linked with John of Gaunt and the Temple in the Inns of Court, seat of the hated lawyers. They threatened to storm the Tower of London itself unless the king met them. When the 14 year old rode into the heart of the peasants at Mile End, they presented him with a series of demands, including the abolition of serfdom and pardons for the rebels. The king agreed and returned to the Tower, only to find that a mob had stormed the building—the drawbridge had been left down—and beheaded the officials they found there, including the hated Lord Chancellor Simon of Sudbury, and Sir Robert Hales, the Lord Treasurer who had introduced the poll tax.

WAT TYLER CONFRONTS RICHARD II

Further discussions were arranged for the next day at Smithfield, closer to the heart of London. This time, the king and his attendants wore chain mail beneath their clothes in case of trouble. Against the advice of other rebel leaders, Wat Tyler rode forwards to talk to the king alone. What the men discussed is not known, but Tyler dismounted and—according to some contemporary accounts—was ill-tempered and rude. He is said to have drawn his dagger, at which point two of the king's party drew their swords. One cut Tyler's neck, the other ran his stomach through, killing him.

With their leader dead, the peasant army was on the verge of charging when

Richard II showed great courage. Riding forward, he called out to them: "Sirs, will you shoot your king? I will be your chief and captain; you shall have from me that which you seek. Only follow me to the

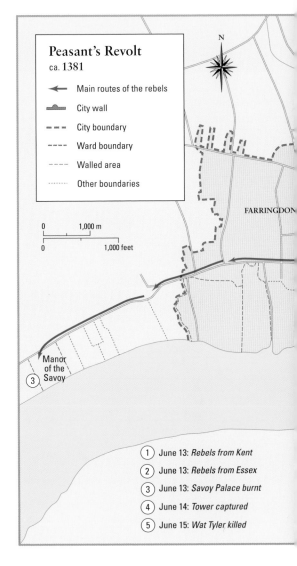

A map of the city of London and the main routes taken by the rebels in the Peasants' revolt of 1381.

Peasant's Revolt
ca. 1381

← Main routes of the rebels
City wall
- - - City boundary
---- Ward boundary
---- Walled area
.... Other boundaries

FARRINGDON

0   1,000 m
0   1,000 feet

Manor of the Savoy ③

① June 13: *Rebels from Kent*
② June 13: *Rebels from Essex*
③ June 13: *Savoy Palace burnt*
④ June 14: *Tower captured*
⑤ June 15: *Wat Tyler killed*

fields without." He then led them toward Clerkenwell, while his lords rounded up a militia that broke up the mob and seized its ringleaders, many of whom were executed. The revolt ended in failure,

and serfdom survived for at least another century. However, the authorities have learnt how dangerous it was to impose the greatest burden of taxation on the lowest members of society.

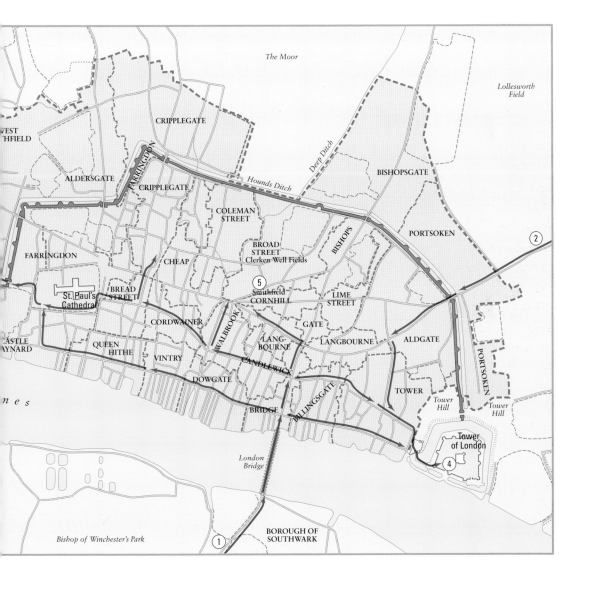

Battle of Agincourt

FOR THE ENGLISH, THE BATTLE OF AGINCOURT WAS A FAMOUS VICTORY FOR THEIR RENOWNED ARCHERS. FOR THE DEFEATED FRENCH, HOWEVER, IT WAS A MILITARY DISASTER MADE WORSE BY THE FACT THAT IT COULD EASILY HAVE BEEN AVOIDED.

The mythology of Agincourt echoes across centuries of English history. The battle forms the centerpiece of Shakespeare's 1599 play *Henry V*, in which the king famously rallies his men:

"And gentlemen in England now a-bed
Shall think themselves accursed they were
not here,
And hold their manhoods cheap whiles any
speaks
That fought with us upon Saint Crispin's
day."

The battle was part of the Hundred Years' War, the struggle between English and French monarchs for dominance of areas of France and Burgundy to which they both laid claim (in fact, the war lasted 116 years, from 1337 to the final French victory in 1453). This latest phase of the war began in 1415, when King Henry V of England sailed to France to recover what he believed was his birthright, the Duchy of Normandy. The territory had last been in English hands more than two hundred years earlier, before the French king had taken it from his vassal, King John of England. Now Henry V assembled an army of some 2,500 men-at-arms (mounted knights in armor, the elite of Europe's warriors) accompanied by 8,000 archers, various servants, and 200 special gunners.

In some ways, Henry V's invasion of France with such a small army seemed like a desperate gamble, but it had three factors going for it. First was the undoubted superiority of English soldiers, particularly the archers. Second, Henry himself was an energetic commander. Third, and most importantly, the French were split by bitter personal and political disputes. King Charles VI held only weak authority. In the power vacuum that existed in France at the time, two groups of nobles—the

A map outlining the tactics employed by the English forces against those of the French at Agincourt. The use of the English longbowmen was a significant element in the success achieved that day.

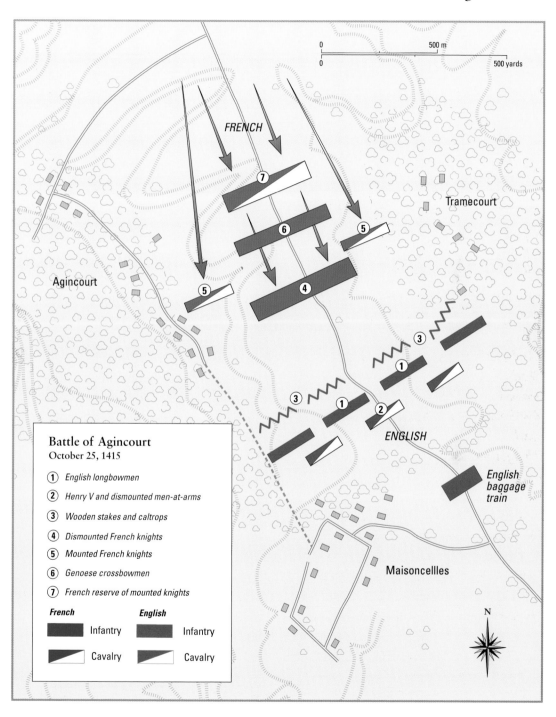

FRENCH

Tramecourt

Agincourt

ENGLISH

English
baggage
train

Maisoncellles

Battle of Agincourt
October 25, 1415

1 English longbowmen

2 Henry V and dismounted men-at-arms

3 Wooden stakes and caltrops

4 Dismounted French knights

5 Mounted French knights

6 Genoese crossbowmen

7 French reserve of mounted knights

French

Infantry

Cavalry

English

Infantry

Cavalry

N

Henry V of England was an energetic leader, which contributed to the success enjoyed by the English on the fateful day. The French, in contrast, were split by bitter personal and political conflict.

THE MARCH TO CALAIS

Henry's forces first captured Harfleur and then set out to march to his own possession, Calais, where he could receive supplies. The small force was shadowed by the far larger French army as they tried to find a place to cross the river Somme. Eventually, the English crossed the river at a marshy ford where the water was only waist deep. The English were by now exhausted, short of food, and demoralized. The French had gone on ahead to block the Calais road near the village of Agincourt. As the English huddled in whatever shelter they could find just down the road in Maisoncelles, many prayed and took confession. They had seen the tracks left by the huge French army, and they knew the odds were against their surviving the next day. The following morning, the armies took up their positions—and there they stayed. The English had to get past the French in order to survive, so would have to fight despite the odds. The French had no need to make the first move. They planned to

Burgundians and the Armagnacs—vied for supremacy. The best available French commander to face the English, John the Fearless of Burgundy, was excluded from the court altogether. This disunity and lack of collective purpose was to prove fatal for the French when they took to the field—in spite of their superior numbers.

neutralize the English archers by a massed cavalry charge of men-at-arms, who would emerge from behind the French line and smash into the enemy's right flank while a smaller cavalry force attacked the left flank. Infantry, including men-at-arms fighting on foot, would attack the middle of the English line. The French archers were deployed behind the line, too far back to make much impression on the fighting. Many spent the battle simply waiting in a nearby field.

THE FRENCH PLANS GO AWRY

After about three hours of waiting, Henry led the English slowly forward to within range of the enemy. Defeat must have seemed inevitable. But as soon as the French launched their charge, it became clear that something had gone wrong with their plan. During the long delay, many men-at-arms had wandered off. Rather than the 1,600 horsemen on the left and 800 on the right, the French could muster only 150 and about 300 respectively. The ground was soft plowed earth, so the horses could not raise much speed. And the battlefield was far too narrow for the French plan to work. The ends of the English lines were in woods, making them impossible to outflank. The French charge was easily beaten back. As it retreated, it crashed into the advancing foot soldiers, causing chaos. The dismounted men-at-arms pressed on, but became exhausted crossing the churned-up ground. They advanced into the setting sun, out of which the English archers fired a hail of arrows that, within about 900 ft (275 m), began to pierce French armor and helmets. Soon the French were being slaughtered in fierce hand-to-hand fighting. The death toll was made far worse when Henry decreed that all prisoners except the highest born should be put to death.

A generation of French nobles and knights died, some 600 in all, including many of the king's most important political allies. Five dukes, twelve counts, and many other nobles were taken captive. The French military and political establishment had been decapitated and its power weakened, and Henry's victory was assured. The final irony was that during the battle, while the English archers cemented their reputation and their place in history, the French archers were barely used behind the lines.

> *Five dukes, twelve counts, and many other nobles were taken captive. The French military and political establishment had been decapitated and its power weakened ...*

The New World

CHRISTOPHER COLUMBUS DIED AN UNHAPPY MAN, BELIEVING HIS CAREER HAD BEEN A FAILURE. HE HAD FAILED TO FIND A WESTERN SEA ROUTE TO ASIA—THE STATED PURPOSE OF HIS JOURNEYS OF DISCOVERY—AND HAD LOST CONTROL OF HISPANIOLA, THE COLONY HE FOUNDED. HISTORY HAS JUDGED HIM DIFFERENTLY.

Columbus was born in Genoa, Italy, in 1451. He became a sailor in his teens and traveled widely, eventually making his base in Portugal. He unsuccessfully approached the Portuguese, English, and French crowns for support for an expedition to discover a westward sea route to the Indies. Asia, particularly China, India, and the Spice Islands were prized for their spices and silk. Traveling by sea would mean that merchants would no longer be subjected to the high tariffs charged along the overland "Silk Road" route across the Middle East and Central Asia.

> *Back in Spain Columbus was made admiral of the Seven Seas and viceroy of the Indies for his achievements. He made three further voyages...*

SEARCH FOR THE WESTERN ROUTE

Portuguese sailors had already discovered a sea route to Asia, sailing via the Cape of Good Hope to India in 1488. However, Columbus believed that there was a shorter western route—despite popular modern belief, all thinking people of the time knew the earth was round. When no patronage was forthcoming, he turned to the ambitious monarchs of Spain, King Ferdinand and Queen Isabella. Eager to overtake their European rivals and gain control of the lucrative spice market, the pair agreed to sponsor an expedition.

But Columbus' calculations were all wrong. He believed that the earth was much smaller than it actually is: with a circumference of around 18,600 miles (30,000 km), rather than the true distance of 24,850 miles (40,000 km). In addition, he thought that Asia was far bigger than it really is, and spread so far around the globe that its eastern part—Japan—was only 2,485 miles (4,000 km) west of Spain.

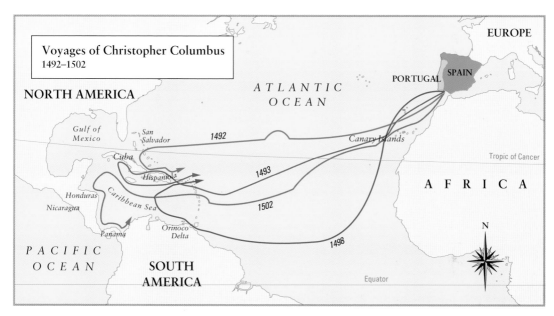

Columbus undertook a series of voyages of discovery, the first of which took place in 1492 with three small ships. In spite of his sense of failure, the discoveries would have a profound effect on the course of history for several powerful European kingdoms including Spain, Portugal, and England.

In fact, Japan is 12,400 miles (20,000 km) from Spain. When Columbus reached the Americas, there was still a whole Pacific Ocean between him and Asia. But what Columbus did understand fully and what helped enormously on his journeys were the "trade winds," which he used both to sail to the Americas and back home again.

MISTAKEN IDENTITIES

On September 6, 1492, Columbus sailed west from the Canary Islands with three ships, and on October 12 spotted land. He disembarked on an island in what is now the Bahamas, which he named San Salvador, before sailing on through the Bahamas to Cuba and on to Hispaniola.

Columbus thought he had reached Japan or China, which he had read about in the memoirs of the Venetian traveler Marco Polo, and so sent his men to look for the emperor's capital, but they found only villages of huts.

Back in Spain, Columbus was made "admiral of the Seven Seas" and viceroy of the Indies for his achievements. He made three further voyages—all under the misapprehension that he was exploring the Indies. The second voyage left the Canary Islands on October 13, 1493, this time with 17 ships and 1,200 men, including priests, farmers, and soldiers, intended to establish

colonies and convert the local people. Taking a more southerly route across the Atlantic, Columbus sailed through the Lesser Antilles, sighted the Virgin Islands, and landed in Puerto Rico. He returned to Hispaniola, where a permanent colony was established,

A replica of Christopher Columbus' ship Santa Maria, *one of the three vessels from the first voyage of discovery undertaken by Columbus in 1492.*

and then sailed to southern Cuba, convinced that it was part of the peninsula attached to mainland China.

The third voyage, in 1498, consisted of just six ships, of which three sailed to the colony on Hispaniola with much-needed provisions for the colonists.

Columbus took the other three ships south of the Caribbean islands to look for a passage to continental Asia. When he reached the South American coastline in Venezuela, near the Orinoco Delta, Columbus realized he had reached a continental landmass,because of the large amount of freshwater flowing from the river. He just didn't know which continent. Unfortunately, back in Hispaniola his settlers were revolting. They accused him of misleading them about the wealth of the new land. Ferdinand and Isabella removed Columbus as governor and he was returned to Spain in chains.

THE FINAL VOYAGE

Eventually, Columbus was freed to undertake his fourth and final voyage in 1502 in search of the Strait of Malacca in the Indian Ocean. Instead, he reached the coastline of Central America and spent two months exploring the coasts of Honduras, Nicaragua, and Costa Rica. Arriving in Panama, Columbus heard stories from the local people about gold and a strait that led to another ocean. He found neither, but it was the first suggestion of the existence of the Pacific Ocean. Instead, he finally returned to Spain in 1504, dying some 18 months later, convinced that his journeys had been wasted.

Whether by accident or design, Columbus had "discovered" a new continent (although millions of people already lived there and would suffer greatly both from the conquests of the Europeans and from the diseases they brought with them). His assumptions and his geography may have been wrong, but his achievement was undeniable—a lesser sailor would have been unable to make the journey.

FACT FILE
Voyages of Christopher Columbus

Dates: 1492; 1493; 1498; 1502

Destination: Route to the Indies

Discoveries: Failed to find a route to the Spice Islands, but discovered the Caribbean islands of San Salvador, Cuba, and Hispaniola on first voyage

Accomplishments: Established colonies, and then discovered the continental landmass of South and Central America

Aftermath: The land was claimed for Spain and resulted in great riches for the Spanish crown for centuries

Bonfire of the Vanities

AT THE END OF THE 15TH CENTURY, FLORENCE WAS ONE OF THE LEADING CENTERS OF THE RENAISSANCE. BUT FOR THREE YEARS IN THE 1490S, FLORENTINES MADE A COLLECTIVE MISTAKE, ALLOWING THE CITY TO FALL UNDER THE INFLUENCE OF SAVONAROLA, WHO WAS FUNDAMENTALLY OPPOSED TO WHAT HE SAW AS "VANITIES."

Born in 1452 in Ferrara, Savonarola became convinced as a young man that the clergy of the Catholic Church had lost touch with the true spirit of their faith. Such concerns remained even after he became a Dominican friar in Bologna in 1475.

Savonarola was far from alone. Many Catholics questioned the immense wealth of the Church and the worldly concerns of the popes and cardinals in Rome, with their personal fortunes, political ambitions, and carnal appetites. Throughout Italy, the faithful joined religious orders in an attempt to renew the spiritual purity of the faith. In 1517, the dissatisfaction would find voice in Martin Luther, resulting in the cataclysm of the Reformation and the splitting of the Church.

> *Many preachers, mystics, monks and nuns claimed to have had warnings that humanity must change its ways, [and] turn its back on "vanities"...*

SAVONAROLA ARRIVES IN FLORENCE

Savonarola's first visit to Florence in the 1480s went virtually unnoticed. However, he carried on denouncing what he saw as faults within the Church and also predicted the imminent end of the world. Again, Savonarola was not alone. Many preachers, mystics, monks, and nuns claimed to have had warnings that humanity must change its ways, turn its back on "vanities", anything that could be construed as luxuries or signs of moral turpitude, and adopt a spiritual rather than a worldly outlook. But when Savonarola was invited back to Florence in 1490, by the leading Renaissance philosopher Giovanni Pico della Mirandola, he was in the right place at the right time.

This statue of Savonarola sculpted by Enrico Pazzi in 1872, sits in front of the Castello Estense in the center of Ferrara. In spite of his past reputation, the Church has recently considered his beatification, and a plaque marks the spot of his execution in Florence. Contemporary scholarship and closer examination of his writings have led to a slight improvement in his notorious reputation.

Florence under Count Lorenzo Medici, known as "the Magnificent," was near the height of its cultural achievement. Lorenzo's glittering court attracted artists such as Leonardo da Vinci, Alessandro Botticelli, and Michelangelo, and thinkers such as della Mirandola and Marsilio Ficino. Lorenzo Medici was intrigued by Savonarola's view of Christianity, but died soon after his arrival in Florence.

In 1494, King Charles VIII of France began a series of wars intended to limit the power of the Habsburgs of the Low Countries and Spain. They were actually fought mainly in Italy, where the city-states made various alliances for or against either side. These French–Italian Wars would last for 65 years, plunging Italy deeper into poverty. The indulgences of the wealthy who patronized the artists, architects, and scholars of the Renaissance became an increasing affront to Savonarola and many of those who crowded into church to hear his hellfire sermons.

A NEW LEADER

One of Charles' first targets was Florence, where he drove out the new Medici ruler Piero "the Unfortunate," in 1494. In the resulting political vacuum, Florentines turned to Savonarola for guidance. The preacher, whose message was just one among many, emerged as the political and spiritual leader of one of Italy's major cities. He declared Florence a republic and began to make new laws that reflected the path he saw as the only way toward spiritual salvation.

Savonarola limited trade, which he saw as a sign of worldly greed; he denounced the Medici and the other ruling families in Italy; and, above all, he attacked Pope Alexander VI, claiming that he alone was appointed by God to lead the Church back to the true faith. In turn, Alexander summoned Savonarola to explain himself. When the priest ignored him, Alexander condemned Savonarola as a heretic.

Within Florence, Savonarola remained a popular figure, and among those who enthusiastically followed him was the artist Botticelli. At the same time, many ordinary people found the strict lifestyle he espoused increasingly difficult to follow because the city's trade began to stagnate and its poverty worsened.

The high point of Savonarola's rule came on February 7, 1497, when his followers held a vast "Bonfire of the Vanities." Ritual burnings of objects associated with sin had taken place early in the 15th century, but Savonarola's bonfire was on an entirely new scale. His followers went through the city, removing any possessions that might be associated with anything other than the purest of morals.

That meant erotic paintings or statues—of course—but also the works of pre-Christian writers, including philosophers such as Aristotle. It also meant anything to do with personal appearance, such as fine clothes, makeup, and even mirrors, and anything to do with idle leisure, such as playing cards and musical instruments. It was like a 15th-century version of the brutal rule enforced by the Taliban in Afghanistan at the end of the 20th century, where many works of art were destroyed, including some rare and ancient statues of the Buddha.

Thousands of irreplaceable objects went up in smoke, including several priceless works of art by Fra Bartolomeo, Lorenzo di Credi, and others, and books of poems by Boccaccio. Botticelli was said to have thrown several of his own works into the flames (the great biographer Giorgio Vasari reported that Botticelli was so persuaded by Savonarola's message that he abandoned painting all together—and thus rendered himself destitute).

SAVONAROLA'S DOWNFALL

By now, most Florentines had had enough. They were no better off than they were under the Medici and, in fact, the economic decline had in many ways made it worse. Opposition to Savonarola's rule grew. In May 1497, disorder spread throughout the city as Florentines began to disobey Savonarola's edicts, openly dancing, singing, and gambling.

The vanities had triumphed. A few days later, Pope Alexander VI excommunicated Savonarola, further weakening his position. The preacher managed to cling on for nearly a year before Alexander had him arrested and charged with heresy and sedition. After being tortured on the rack, Savonarola and two colleagues confessed to heresy and were sentenced to death. They were hung in chains from a cross and burnt to death on May 23, 1498, on the very spot where the "Bonfire of the Vanities" had taken place. A plaque now commemorates the place of execution in Florence. The Florentine Republic limped on with French support until 1512, when the Medici finally returned to the city with Spanish backing.

FACT FILE
Bonfire of the Vanities

Date: February 7, 1497

Location: Florence, Italy

Historical Context: French–Italian Wars (1494–1498); widespread poverty

Central Figure: Girolamo Savonarola, political and spiritual leader of the Florentine Republic

Chain of Events: Charles drove the Medici ruler out of Florence; Savonarola emerged as the city's political leader, declared it a republic, and limited trade; 'Bonfire of the Vanities' (1497)

Aftermath: Thousands of irreplaceable objects were destroyed. Savonarola lost public support and was executed on May 23, 1498

"Thousands of irreplaceable objects went up in smoke, including several priceless works of art by Fra Bartolomeo, Lorenzo di Credi, and others, and books of poems by Boccaccio."

Early Modern World

The world entered an age of conquest, exploration, and conflict. The demise of the Aztec and Inca civilizations, the collapse of the Easter island populations, and failure of early settlements in North America had far-reaching consequences. The defeat of the Spanish Armada and the loss of the American colonies through revolution were the result of disastrous mistakes on a national scale, while the Great Fire of London, the Salem Witch Trials, and the Scilly naval disaster were the result of human error on a smaller scaler. More personal mistakes were committed in the cases of Henry Hudson and Lady Jane Grey, with dire results for both.

Cortés and the Aztec

IN JUST 200 YEARS, THE AZTEC TRIBE OF NORTH MEXICO HAD CONQUERED AN EMPIRE THAT COVERED MUCH OF WHAT IS NOW MEXICO. FROM THEIR VAST CAPITAL AT TENOCHTITLÁN (NOW MEXICO CITY), THEY RULED THEIR SUBJECT PEOPLES IN A SYSTEM BASED ON TRIBUTE AND HUMAN SACRIFICE.

The mighty empire was overthrown, however, in just two years by a few hundred Spanish adventurers led by Hernán Cortés. He was one of a new generation of adventurers eager to gain status and wealth from the new lands discovered by Spanish seafarers in the early part of the 16th century. These conquistadors extended Spain's empire while pursuing personal glory.

Historians have long puzzled over how the conquistador was able to bring down Moctezuma, a fearsome and brave warrior, with comparative ease.

When Cortés set sail from the Spanish province of Cuba in February 1519, he was officially searching for survivors of an earlier Spanish expedition to present-day Mexico. But his real motive was to investigate stories of the region's untold riches of precious metals and jewels. Cortés and some 600 men landed in present-day Veracruz, Mexico, in April 1519.

Cortés then sank all but one of his ships, forcing his men to stay with him, and headed inland. They quickly defeated the local Tlaxcala, a victory that would have immense strategic importance. As the Tlaxcala were sworn enemies of the Aztec, they became the Spaniards' allies.

GROWTH OF THE AZTEC EMPIRE

The Aztec had settled on the site of Tenochtitlán in the 13th century and began a remarkable rise to power by first working as mercenaries for the warring cities of the region, and then using their military power to turn against and conquer their employers. Aztec society was based on a warrior elite, and their military prowess enabled them to expand throughout the whole of what is now central Mexico. Conquered peoples were absorbed into the growing empire and forced to pay 'tribute' to the Aztec in the form of labor and food, and were also expected to supply the captives for one of the most renowned aspects of Aztec life: human sacrifice.

By August 1521—just two years after his arrival—Cortés and his 600 men had destroyed a vast empire that stretched across Mexico and had existed for 200 years. Historians have long puzzled over how the conquistador was able to bring down the Aztec emperor Moctezuma, a fearsome and brave warrior, with comparative ease. But the Spaniards did have two powerful weapons—the horse and firearms. Both would prove decisive.

Cortés and his Tlaxcala allies took advantage of the fragmented nature of the empire, and of resentment against the Aztec rulers, to gather allies. Along the way, he acquired a translator—and a mistress—in the shape of Doña Marina, a Nahua slave.

Moctezuma met Cortés and gave him gifts in the hope of dissuading him from continuing his journey, but they only made the Spaniard more determined to reach the capital of this wealthy empire. Moctezuma's failure may have also reflected an Aztec belief that one of their gods, Quetzalcóatl, would return from across the sea—he may have believed the Spanish leader was the fulfillment of this prophecy.

Cortés arrived at the Aztec capital, Tenochtitlán on November 8, 1519, supported by 1,000 Tlaxcala. Moctezuma treated the Spaniards as visiting dignitaries. The Spanish were overwhelmed by the sight, size, and wealth of the Aztec capital, which far outshone any contemporary European city. Cortés, however, was mindful that at any moment he might be taken prisoner: Tenochtitlán was built on islands connected to the shore by causeways and bridges. In a bold move, he cajoled Moctezuma to take up residency in the Spaniards' quarters.

MOCTEZUMA BECOMES CORTÉS' "GUEST"

For the months Montezuma remained the "guest" of the Spanish visitors, his power was severely reduced. Yet Cortés was unable to exploit the power vacuum, because he had to contend with a rival Spanish expedition sent to take him back to Cuba to answer a charge of overstepping his authority. While Cortés and most of his men were defeating the newly arrived Spaniards, just 80 men were left in charge of Tenochtitlán. Cortés returned to find them and the emperor under siege. With the food markets closed and Moctezuma's power gone, order had slipped away. The emperor's brother Cuitláhuac, gathered an army to challenge the Spaniards. During the battle that followed, Moctezuma

was mortally wounded. The Spaniards
fled Tenochtitlán but two-thirds of the
conquistadors were killed as they fled along
the causeways, laden down with gold bars.

THE CONQUISTADOR CONQUERS

With Moctezuma's death, Cortés saw an
opportunity to take control. With the
backing of his Tlaxcala allies, he fought
a series of battles against the Aztec. The
Spaniards had the upper hand with
superior weapons, cannons, and guns.
Cortés was a skilled commander and his
men better disciplined than their enemy.

In February 1521, Cuitláhuac was
installed as emperor. Cortés decided to
lay siege to Tenochtitlán to force the
Aztec surrender. He ordered ships built to
blockade the city's canals, preventing any
food from being brought in. The Spaniards
also cut off the fresh water supply. The
Aztecs attempted to fight back, but, after
75 days of siege, the last Aztec emperor
surrendered on August 3. 1521, and
the Aztec empire ceased to exist. Cortés
became Marques of the Valley of Oaxaca,
but King Charles V of Spain sent another
nobleman to rule the colony as viceroy.
The Aztec became subject to the growing
Spanish empire.

*Cortés' conquest of the Aztec empire, and its subsequent fall remains
somewhat of a mystery, given the huge number of Aztec and the small
number of Spanish troops.*

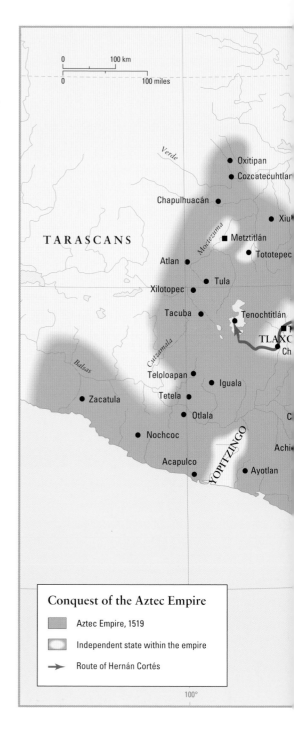

Conquest of the Aztec Empire

Aztec Empire, 1519

Independent state within the empire

→ Route of Hernán Cortés

Tropic of Cancer

Gulf of Mexico

uxpan

Y u c a t á n

20°

apa

Veracruz ●

Mixtlan ●

Tochtepec ●   ● Ucila

Totoltepec ●

Chiapan ●   ● Xaltepec

axaca ●   ● Mitla

Grijalva

Tehuantepec ●

epec

LITY OF TOTOTEPEC

Mapachtepec ●

■ Soconusco

Soconusco

● Huiztlan

S. de Minas

15°

● Mazatlán

● Ayotlan

N

P A C I F I C   O C E A N

95°

90°

End of an Empire

THE STORY OF HOW A MIGHTY SOUTH AMERICAN EMPIRE WITH A POPULATION OF AT LEAST FIVE MILLION PEOPLE COULD BE TOPPLED BY A MOTLEY COLLECTION OF JUST 200 SPANIARDS IS ONE OF HISTORY'S MORE EXTRAORDINARY TALES.

By the time the Spaniards arrived in South America, the Inca empire stretched from what is now northern Chile to southern Colombia and took in Peru, Bolivia, Ecuador, and parts of Argentina. Cusco, a sophisticated city of stone buildings and gold statues, served as the religious, political, administrative, and cultural capital, and was linked by an extensive road network to the empire's provinces. Inca society was highly stratified: at its peak was the Inca Sapa, the absolute ruler whom the Inca believed was a direct descendant of the sun god Inti. The empire he controlled was based on the subjugation of conquered peoples, who were made subject to Inca laws, obliged to pay taxes in the form of labor, and in return were fed and housed. Many were unhappy under Inca rule and the Spanish exploited this discontent.

> *Cusco, a sophisticated city of stone buildings and gold statues, served as the religious, political, administrative, and cultural capital ...*

FIRST ENCOUNTERS

Conquistador Francisco Pizarro was one of the foremost Spanish adventurers for whom the quest to find the fabled riches of South America had become an obsession. Pizarro (ca. 1471–1541) had returned home empty-handed from a first voyage to the New World in November 1524. His second voyage was far larger, involving 160 men and some horses. Pizarro split the expedition, sending his pilot Bartolomé Ruiz to explore the coast of present-day Ecuador, where he encountered the Inca for the first time. Ruiz was amazed by their gold and silver jewelry, precious stones, and beautifully woven fabrics.

Ruiz and Pizarro were reunited and using three Inca as interpreters, they sailed

Pizarro's conquest of the Inca empire took place as a result of a series of expeditions and encounters.

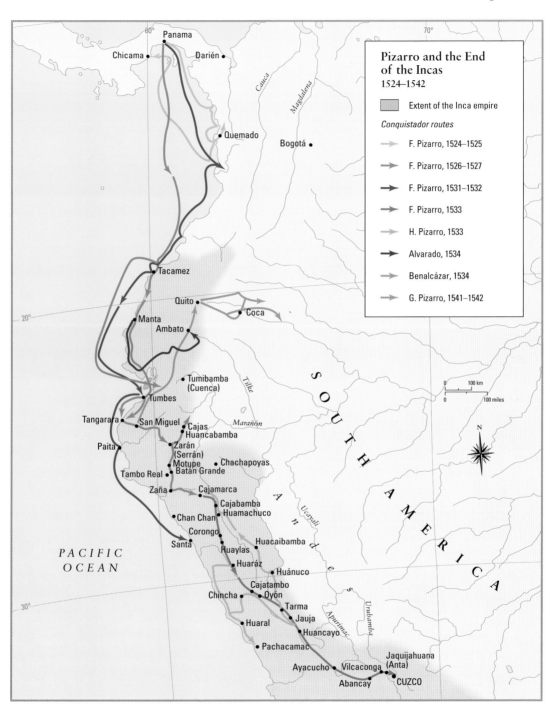

Pizarro and the End
of the Incas
1524–1542

Extent of the Inca empire

Conquistador routes

F. Pizarro, 1524–1525

F. Pizarro, 1526–1527

F. Pizarro, 1531–1532

F. Pizarro, 1533

H. Pizarro, 1533

Alvarado, 1534

Benalcázar, 1534

G. Pizarro, 1541–1542

The ruins of Machu Picchu, an Inca city in the Cusco district built for the Emperor Pachicuti (1438–1472). It was never visited by the Spanish conquerors, so it remained unknown to the outside world until it was written about by American historian Hiram Bingham in 1911. It is an important archaeological site, and is much visited by tourists from around the globe.

south, where Ruiz had been told the gold originated. At Tumbes on the Peruvian coast, the Spaniards were welcomed by the local governor, who sent word of their arrival to the Sapa Wayna Capac. Wayna Capac learnt that his empire had been hit by smallpox, a disease unknown to the Inca (probably introduced by Europeans). Within days, many of the king's trusted generals were dead and Wayna Capac himself was sick.

When Wayna Capac died, a civil war broke out as his sons Atahualpa and Huascar fought for control of the empire. Pizarro hurried back to Spain, where he showed King Charles V the gold and other goods he had obtained in Peru. The king was impressed enough to send Pizarro back to South America under a royal licence "to discover and conquer Peru." The job was easier than Pizarro could have dared hope.

The following year Pizarro and his men (62 cavalry and 102 infantrymen) sailed back to Tumbes. They found the city ransacked and the empire wracked by civil war. The Spaniards marched into the interior; although Atahualpa followed their progress, he was less concerned with stopping them than with monitoring the movements of his brother Huascar. It was a fatal mistake. As he made his way inland, Pizarro was recruiting enemies of the Inca.

Atahualpa was resting at Cajamarca after a battle when an advance party of Spaniards arrived to arrange a meeting between him and Pizarro. The encounter on November 16, 1532 was hostile. According to Inca accounts, the Spaniards poured away welcome drinks offered to them. Spanish accounts say that Atahualpa threw away a Bible offered to him. The stage was set for a confrontation.

TAKEN HOSTAGE

At a prearranged signal from Pizarro, the Spaniards attacked Atahualpa's entourage and seized the emperor from under the noses of 80,000 Inca warriors. Taken hostage, Atahualpa attempted to negotiate his freedom. He offered his captors a ransom of a room entirely filled with gold and two of silver. He had Huascar killed so that he could not offer a higher ransom to get the Spanish to hold onto their hostage.

However, Atahualpa had massively underestimated the greed of the Spaniards. In their minds, Atahualpa's willingness to part with so much was proof that there must be more gold and silver available.

AN EMPIRE CRUMBLES

The Spaniards tried Atahualpa on the pretext of his brother's death and accusations that he had plotted against Pizarro. Found guilty, he was executed on July 26, 1533. With no Inca Sapa at its head, the empire fell apart. A year later, Pizarro conquered the capital Cusco, using troops drawn from the Inca's subject peoples. Pizarro could not believe the splendour of the city. He wrote to the king, Charles V, "This city is the greatest and the finest ever seen in this country or anywhere in the Indies...it is so beautiful and has such fine buildings that it would be remarkable even in Spain."

The largest empire in pre-Columbian America had fallen to the Spanish invaders, but in truth it held the seeds of its own downfall. Its high degree of centralization meant that it was vulnerable if the center fell; the removal of the Sapa Inca as absolute ruler left a power vacuum. Furthermore, the Inca had no resistance to the smallpox, and its arrival must have terrified them. Pizarro had the good fortune to arrive at a time of civil war, when the provinces' conquered populations provided recruits for his forces. In battle, the Spaniards had distinct advantages. Horses had never been seen in the empire, while the Spaniards' guns and mechanical crossbows also proved lethal.

Lady Jane Grey

TODAY IN THE UK, THE PHRASE "NINE-DAY WONDER" IS USED TO DESCRIBE ANY SHORT-LIVED SUCCESS. ITS ROOTS LIE IN ONE OF THE ODDEST EPISODES OF THE TUDOR AGE, WHEN A YOUNG WOMAN, MUCH AGAINST HER WILL, WAS PUT ON THE THRONE AS QUEEN OF ENGLAND FOR JUST NINE DAYS. SHE WAS OVERTHROWN AND BEHEADED, PAYING A TRAGIC PRICE FOR THE MISTAKES OF THE PLOTTERS WHO HAD HER CROWNED.

Lady Jane Grey was probably born in October 1537, the same month as the rightful heir to the English crown, Edward VI. She was the eldest daughter of Henry Grey, who would become the first Duke of Suffolk in 1551, while her mother, Lady Frances Brandon, was a granddaughter of King Henry VII. That made Jane and her two younger sisters grandnieces of the then ruler, Henry VIII.

In 1546, Jane was sent to court to serve Henry's sixth wife, Katherine Parr. By all accounts, Jane was a dutiful girl and a fierce adherent to Protestantism, which had become established in England after Henry VIII's first divorce and split from the Roman Catholic Church in the 1530s.

Jane was sent to court to serve Henry's sixth wife, Katherine Parr. By all accounts, Jane was a dutiful girl and a fierce adherent to Protestantism.

REGENCY RULE

Henry VIII died on January 28, 1547 and was succeeded by his only son, Edward VI. As the young king was not yet ten, a Regency Council ruled on his behalf, led first by his uncle Edward Seymour, Duke of Somerset, and later by John Dudley, the Earl of Warwick and later Duke of Northumberland.

On May 25, 1553, Lady Jane married Lord Guildford Dudley, John Dudley's son. The young king was now terminally ill with tuberculosis and Jane's new father-in-law, his chief counsellor, was the most powerful man in the country. Eager to preserve his power, he had the

Queen for just nine days, the young Lady Jane Grey lost her head through no fault of her own.

Regency Council draw up a "Devise for the Succession," which named Jane, Edward's cousin, as his successor and heir, excluding Edward's half-sisters Mary and Elizabeth from the succession. Less than a month later Edward VI was dead.

A NEW QUEEN
On July 9, 1553, Lady Jane Grey was called before the Council and informed that she would be the new queen. At no point had Lady Jane sought to become monarch, but her Protestant faith led to her becoming a pawn in the religious conflicts of the Reformation. Edward's brief reign had shored up the position of the Protestant Church of England established by his father. Guided by the Archbishop of Canterbury Thomas Cranmer, the king had allowed reforms, such as the printing of the Book of Common Prayer in English rather than Latin, reinforcing the break with the Catholic Church in Rome. Many officials in the government and senior churchmen had no wish to go back. Edward himself may have been instrumental in making Jane his heir to ensure that his half-sister and natural heir, the Catholic princess Mary, would never sit on the throne.

John Dudley declared Lady Jane the new Queen of England on July 10, 1553. She is alleged to have said, "The crown is not my right and pleaseth me not. The Lady Mary is the rightful heir." Jane moved to the Tower of London, the traditional home of the expectant heir, but her appointment was met with disquiet beyond the Tower walls. The general populace had expected Mary to become the next queen; many still had great affection for the "old religion" and few knew of this cousin who was about to become queen.

THE RIGHTFUL HEIR MARCHES
Over the next nine days, Lady Jane Grey's fate was sealed. On hearing the news of her succession, Mary set off from East Anglia to London with an army to claim her throne. Lady Jane also used her new authority to refuse to make her husband, Guildford Dudley, king, despite pressure from his family.

On July 11, the sermon at St. Paul's Cathedral declared Jane to be queen and the princesses Mary and Elizabeth to be illegitimate, with no claim to the throne. But within days it was clear Jane did not have popular support. Guildford Dudley was sent to meet Mary with an army of just 600, but while Mary's support was growing, Jane's was ebbing away. Her father and father-in-law were squabbling about whether Dudley should become king. The members of the Regency Council deserted her, announcing their support for Mary. Only her father and the Archbishop of Canterbury Cranmer continued to support Jane—and then Cranmer switched sides.

THE RELUCTANT QUEEN

On the ninth day, Mary was publicly declared queen. Jane begged simply to be allowed to return home, but it was not to be. She and Guildford Dudley were charged with high treason and imprisoned in the Tower of London, where they were found guilty on November 13, 1553, and sentenced to death.

Even then it still seemed possible that Jane would be spared the death penalty. Then, however, news spread of a plan for Queen Mary to wed the Catholic King Philip II of Spain. The aristocrat and poet Sir Thomas Wyatt led a Protestant rebellion against the marriage, which Jane's father and uncles joined.

Jane had had nothing to do with the Protestant rebellion, but it gave Mary an excuse to implicate her. Mary feared that, while she lived, Jane would remain a figurehead for opposition to her rule. She was also troubled that Jane refused to convert to Catholicism.

Jane and her husband were beheaded at the Tower of London on February 12, 1554. Her father-in-law, the Duke of Northumberland, had been executed the previous August, while her father was executed the following week, on February 19. Lady Jane's tragedy was that she never sought to be queen. She was a pawn of ambitious parents and parents-in-law who fatally miscalculated the mood of the English people and the strength of Mary's support. Against this background of religious bigotry and violence, Jane Grey was the ultimate sacrificial lamb—truly, a "nine-day wonder."

FACT FILE

Lady Jane Grey

Born: ca. 1536/37

Birthplace: Broadgate Park, Leicestershire

Historical Role: Queen of England for nine days

Marital Alliances: Lord Guildford Dudley

Historic Feats: Appointed queen by the Regency Council headed by her father-in-law, John Dudley Mary

Died: February 12, 1554, beheaded at the Tower of London

Hero or Villain: More martyr or political pawn than hero or villain

Roanoke, the Lost Colony

BY THE LATE 16TH CENTURY, THE NEW WORLD WAS NO LONGER QUITE SO NEW, AS GENERATIONS HAD PASSED SINCE COLUMBUS HAD CROSSED THE ATLANTIC. THE AMERICAS WERE ATTRACTING EUROPEAN COLONIZATION, BUT FEW ATTEMPTS WENT SO BADLY AS THE ENGLISH SETTLEMENT OF ROANOKE.

The colony was the brainchild of Sir Walter Raleigh, the adventurer, explorer, pirate, and favorite of Queen Elizabeth I. It suited England's political aims to establish a base in the New World, not only because of its rumored wealth, but also to keep pace with Spain, which was establishing a rich overseas empire in South America. And it suited Raleigh's personal aims because an English colony on the North American coast would serve as a base for privateers—pirates in royal service, like Raleigh himself—to raid the Spanish fleets carrying gold from South America back home.

Raleigh had no intention of heading to the New World himself ... so he dispatched and expedition led by sea captains Phillip Amadas and Arthur Barlowe.

THE FIRST SETTLEMENT

In 1584, Elizabeth gave Raleigh a charter, allowing him to set up colonies in what became known as Virginia. Raleigh had no intention of heading to the New World himself—his celebrated voyages came a decade later—so he dispatched an expedition led by sea captains Phillip Amadas and Arthur Barlowe. While exploring off what is now North Carolina, Amadas and Barlowe came across an island about 7½ miles (12 km) long and 2 miles (3 km) wide, which the inhabitants called Roanoke. It seemed promising for settlement, particularly as the local Secotans and Croatoans were friendly. Barlowe returned to England with two Croatoans to persuade Raleigh to fund a further expedition, but this time to establish a military colony.

The position of Roanoke Island, its fateful settlement, and the coast of what would become Virginia.

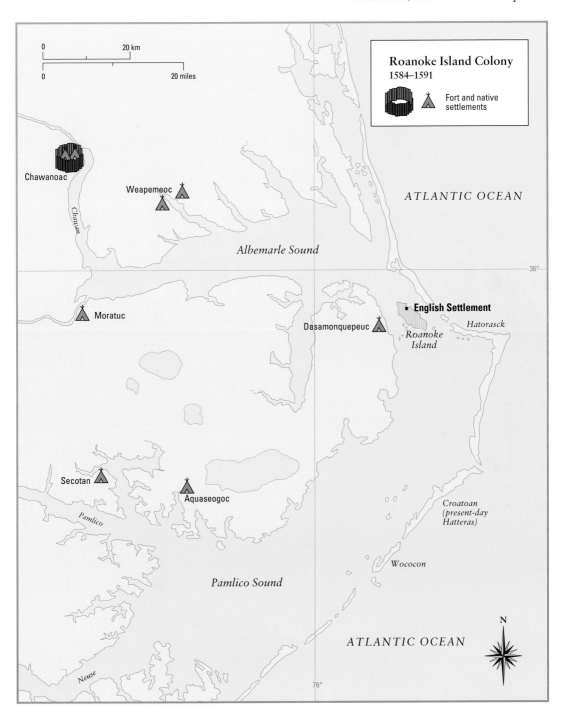

Roanoke Island Colony
1584–1591

Fort and native settlements

ATLANTIC OCEAN

Chawanoac

Chawan

Weapemeoc

Albemarle Sound

36°

Moratuc

Dasamonquepeuc

• **English Settlement**

Hatorasck

Roanoke Island

Secotan

Aquaseogoc

Pamlico

Croatoan (present-day Hatteras)

Wococon

Pamlico Sound

Neuse

ATLANTIC OCEAN

N

76°

0   20 km

0   20 miles

Sir Walter Raleigh, adventurer, explorer, pirate, and great favorite of Queen Elizabeth I, sent an expedition to Virginia.

A fleet of five ships commanded by Sir Richard Grenville reached Roanoke in July. As Grenville's men explored the island, however, a fateful incident occurred. In the village of Aquascogoc, the English realized that a silver cup was missing and accused the locals of stealing it. Grenville had their village destroyed—but he had miscalculated. His intended show of force became instead a source of resentment that cast a shadow over the colony's future.

In August, Grenville departed for England, promising to return the following April with much-needed supplies. He left 107 men under the command of Ralph Lane to build a fort at the northern end of the island. From their base, Lane's men ventured up to 125 miles (200 km) onto the mainland. But in order to get supplies, they often resorted to kidnapping native peoples. Like Grenville, they had little understanding of neighborly relations.

Tensions grew as the colonists' food stocks fell and the date of Grenville's promised return came and went. When another of the great privateers, Sir Francis Drake, called at the island in June 1586 after raiding Spanish ships in the Caribbean, the colonists cut their losses and left with him (their great contribution to history was to take three plants to Europe with which they had become familiar: potatoes, tobacco, and maize). When Grenville arrived shortly afterward, he found the fort abandoned. He left behind 15 men to maintain Raleigh's claim to the colony, then he sailed home.

RECOLONIZING THE COLONY

Raleigh was not about to give up his colonial ambitions. The following year he arranged a new expedition. His friend John White, an artist and a veteran of Grenville's expedition, would become governor of a new colony of 150 settlers on Chesapeake Bay, as well as Grenville's men on Roanoke.

When White's fleet landed at Roanoke, however, there was no sign of the garrison, apart from a single skeleton.

Now White's plans unexpectedly changed when the captain of his fleet refused to continue. So White and his party settled on Roanoke. It was there that the first English child was born in the Americas, Virginia Dare, White's granddaughter. Despite the settlers' friendly overtures, however, the native peoples were now firmly hostile. At the colonists' bidding, White returned to England to recruit more defenders. He left behind some 90 men, 17 women, and 11 children.

White's intention to return almost immediately was thwarted by a combination of political circumstance and bad luck. England was at war with Spain and all shipping had been commandeered to face the Spanish Armada. The two small ships he did manage to get hold of were raided at sea by Spanish privateers.

THE SETTLERS VANISH

It was three years before White could return to Roanoke on August 18, 1590, Virginia Dare's third birthday, with a party of privateers from the Caribbean. There was no sign of the settlers—but neither was there any sign of violence. The houses and the fort had been carefully taken down. White had agreed before he left that if the colonists were attacked by natives, they would carve a cross into a tree—but there was no sign of any cross.

There were only two clues: on a wooden post someone had carved the word "Croatoan," and on a nearby tree were the letters "Cro." Croatoan was the name of both a local people and a nearby island (now called Hatteras). White took the words as a sign that the settlers had moved to the other island, but he could not check. A huge storm was coming and the privateers put to sea before there was any time to make a search.

Twelve years later, in 1602—by which time White himself was dead—Raleigh sent a ship to establish what had happened to the Roanoke settlers. It was thwarted by bad weather. Five years after that, in 1607, the first successful English settlement in North America was founded at Jamestown, Virginia, and the colonial story moved on. No further clues as to the fate of the settlers of Roanoke were ever found, and the legend of the "Lost Colony" took hold.

... the colonial story moved on. No further clues as to the fate of the settlers of Roanoke were ever found, and the legend of the 'Lost Colony' took hold.

Spanish Armada

By the late 16th century, Spain was Europe's dominant power, but its Catholic King Philip II was irritated by Queen Elizabeth I, who both interfered in Spain's American colonies and protected Protestants across Europe.

Philip decided to bring Elizabeth to heel with a demonstration of the strength of his mighty fleet, the armada. It was a demonstration that would end in disaster for Philip. The difficulties between Spain and England dated back to King Henry VIII's first divorce and his break with Rome in 1534, and England's isolation from Catholic Europe. Following Elizabeth's accession to the throne in 1558 on the death of her half-sister Mary I (who reigned 1553–1558), England became resolutely Protestant. Elizabeth sent an army to France to help the Protestant Huguenots, following a massacre of 3,000 Protestants during the French Wars of Religion in 1572, and also supported the Protestant population of the Netherlands in its bid to gain independence from Spain, which then ruled the region.

None of this sat well with Philip, who resolved to stop Elizabeth from meddling in his affairs by marrying her, just as he had married her half-sister Mary in 1554 (the pair had no children). However, the Virgin Queen Elizabeth insisted that she was married only to her country and rejected Philip's proposal.

From 1559 onward, Philip thought about invading England, ostensibly to protect the rights of English Catholics, but was put off by the size of the naval force he would require. However, England's support for the Protestants during the Revolt of the Netherlands caused him to reassess his views. His councillors advised the king to attack as a warning to England to stay out of Spanish business.

The English meanwhile realized that support for a successful revolt in the Netherlands would prevent the Spanish from launching an invasion. Equally, they understood that their help for the Dutch

Routes taken by Spanish and English fleets during the defeat of the Spanish armada, May to September 1559.

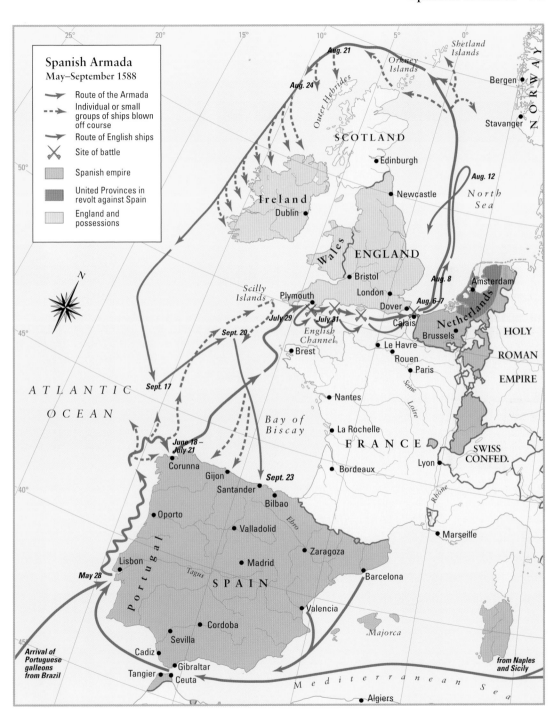

Spanish Armada
May–September 1588

→ Route of the Armada
⇢ Individual or small groups of ships blown off course
→ Route of English ships
✕ Site of battle
▨ Spanish empire
▨ United Provinces in revolt against Spain
▨ England and possessions

Shetland Islands
Aug. 21
Orkney Islands
Bergen
NORWAY
Aug. 24
Outer Hebrides
Stavanger
SCOTLAND
Edinburgh
Aug. 12
Newcastle
North Sea
Ireland
Dublin
Amsterdam
Aug. 8
Wales
ENGLAND
Bristol
London
Netherlands
Scilly Islands
Plymouth
Dover
Aug. 6–7
Brussels
HOLY
July 29
July 31
Calais
ROMAN
Sept. 20
English Channel
Le Havre
EMPIRE
Sept. 17
Brest
Rouen
Paris
ATLANTIC
OCEAN
Seine
Nantes
Loire
June 18 – July 21
Corunna
Bay of Biscay
La Rochelle
FRANCE
SWISS CONFED.
Gijon
Sept. 23
Bordeaux
Lyon
Santander
Bilbao
Oporto
Valladolid
Ebro
Marseille
Zaragoza
Madrid
May 28
Lisbon
Portugal
Tagus
SPAIN
Barcelona
Valencia
Cordoba
Majorca
Arrival of Portuguese galleons from Brazil
Sevilla
Cadiz
Gibraltar
Tangier
Ceuta
from Naples and Sicily
Mediterranean Sea
Algiers

N

4d

ARTIST UNKNOWN c.1575 / HARRISON

The defeat of the Spanish armada confirmed Elizabeth's popularity and the reputation of her naval commander, Sir Francis Drake.

was preoccupied with who would become the next king of Portugal, Spain's neighbor, and its huge colony in Brazil. However, Philip was growing increasingly irritated by the level of English piracy—led by Sir Francis Drake—against Spanish ships in the Caribbean Sea, and so decided to strengthen his maritime force with immediate effect.

Drake's activities in the Caribbean were only one justification for Philip regarding England as an aggressive enemy that must be stopped. Elizabeth's interference in the Netherlands from 1585 was another. A third was Elizabeth's execution of Catholic Mary Queen of Scots in 1587, fearing a plot by English Catholics to free the imprisoned queen.

rebels risked being interpreted by the Spanish as a deliberate provocation. When Philip appointed his half-brother Don John of Austria, a known supporter of an invasion of England, as governor of the Netherlands, the English took it as a clear sign that Philip was planning some kind of military solution.

PLOTS AND PIRACY

In fact, the English were mistaken. Philip had no intention of invading, because he

CONSTRUCTION OF A MIGHTY FLEET

In 1586, Philip ordered the building of an armada, or fleet. It took more than two years, in part because of a raid led by Drake on the Spanish port of Cadiz in April 1587. The 122 ships were finally ready in 1588. Philip proposed that the armada should sail straight from Spain. The Duke of Parma, Philip's governor in the Netherlands, wanted to delay until he could capture a Dutch port from the rebels and bring reinforcements to the armada. But Philip was impatient and ordered the armada to sail straight for Kent.

English ships twice tried to stop the advance of the armada in Spanish waters but were forced back by storms. When the armada did finally appear off Land's End in England in July 1588, the 66-strong British fleet was caught off guard, resupplying in Plymouth. It was said that the English commander Sir Francis Drake, when told of the Spaniards' arrival while he was playing bowls at Plymouth, completed his game before going onboard his vessel and leading the fleet to sea. Elizabeth I rallied her troops in a famous speech, saying "I know I have the body of a weak and feeble woman, but I have the heart of a king, and of a king of England, too."

CLASH IN THE CHANNEL
The two fleets clashed repeatedly in the English Channel. Two Spanish ships were lost, both to accidents. The Spanish admiral, the Duke of Medina Sidonia, then inexplicably chose to anchor at Calais in France, allowing the English to attack the armada. The Spaniards' situation grew worse when storms blew their ships into the North Sea. With their route back through the Channel blocked, the only way home was to sail around the Scotland and Ireland. During this long journey, more ships were lost to tempestuous seas.

Although two-thirds of the armada eventually sailed back to Spain, the damage was done. For the Spanish, the episode had been a naval disaster and a political catastrophe. By ignoring his admirals' advice and making his own plans, Philip had not only failed to make his point with Elizabeth, he had dealt a mortal blow to Spain's military reputation. In England, by contrast, relief was combined with the recognition of the country's new dominance of the seas and a new peak in popularity for Elizabeth I.

FACT FILE
Spanish Armada

Date: July–August 1588

States Involved: England, Spain

Monarchs: Elizabeth I of England; King Philip II of Spain

Numbers: 34 warships, 163 armed merchant vessels, 30 flyboats on English side; 22 Spanish galleons, 108 armed merchant vessels on Spanish side

Outcome: England lost 8 fire ships; Spain lost 5 ships in battle, 51 were wrecked and 10 scuttled

Result: Resounding English victory and humiliation for Spain

Henry Hudson

THE BRITISH EXPLORER AND NAVIGATOR HENRY HUDSON DEDICATED HIS LIFE TO DISCOVERING THE FABLED NORTH-WEST PASSAGE AROUND THE TOP OF NORTH AMERICA TO ASIA. HE PAID THE ULTIMATE PRICE FOR HIS FAILURE TO FIND THE PASSAGE WHEN HIS CREW MUTINIED AND CAST HIM ADRIFT IN A SMALL BOAT IN 1611. HUDSON WAS NEVER FOUND NOR HEARD OF AGAIN.

Little is known of Hudson's early life, including where and when he was born, although it may have been around 1565. It is thought that he sailed as a cabin boy and eventually worked his way up to ship's captain.

In 1607, the Muscovy Trading Company of England hired Hudson to find a north-west sea passage to Asia. Europe's merchants were obsessed with finding a sea route to China and the Spice Islands. The sea route would be quicker than land routes to Asia and would reduce the cost of spices and would also undermine the Islamic states who controlled land routes. The North-west Passage, along the edge of the Arctic Circle, was thought to offer a navigable route for at least part of the year.

> *The North-west Passage, along the edge of the Arctic Circle, was thought to offer a navigable route for at least part of the year.*

THREE VOYAGES, THREE DEAD ENDS

On May 1, 1607, Henry Hudson sailed west on the ageing 80-ton (72-tonne) *Hopewell* with a crew of ten men and a boy. On that first expedition, Hudson traveled to the east coast of Greenland before heading north. Even in June the weather was atrocious, with gales, freezing temperatures, and snow. The ship's rigging froze and heavy fog obscured the visibility. Hudson headed north-east and eventually sighted Spitzbergen. They continued past, spotting many whales some 745 miles (1,200 km) north of the Arctic Circle at what was later called Whales Bay (some people suggest

Henry Hudson's ill-fated final route in search of the North-west Passage. His crew mutinied and set him adrift in a small vessel in Hudson Bay.

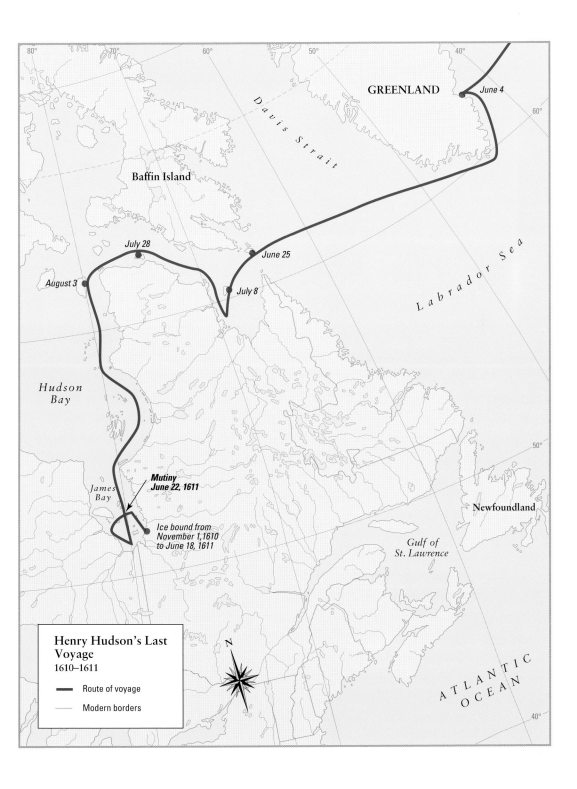

GREENLAND

June 4

Davis Strait

Baffin Island

Labrador Sea

July 28

June 25

August 3

July 8

Hudson
Bay

Newfoundland

Mutiny
June 22, 1611

James
Bay

Ice bound from
November 1,1610
to June 18, 1611

Gulf of
St. Lawrence

N

Henry Hudson's Last
Voyage
1610–1611

———— Route of voyage

⋯⋯⋯ Modern borders

ATLANTIC
OCEAN

that Hudson's reports started the whaling industry in northern waters). At the end of July, when icebergs blocked its sea passage farther north, the ship was forced to turn south and head back to England. As the *Hopewell* sailed south, at approximately 71 degrees north, Hudson named a tiny island after himself. He was, by then, about 400 miles (640 km) off course.

Despite the fact that Hudson had gone in completely the wrong direction, the Muscovy Company commissioned a second voyage. This time Hudson was to attempt to discover an easterly sea route to the Indies, sailing around northern Russia. The *Hopewell* left England in April 1908 and sailed through the Arctic Circle as far as Novaya Zemlya, a distance of 2,500 miles (4,025 km). Once again, ice blocked its passage and the ship was forced to turn back, sailing back to England in late August of that year.

After Hudson's two failed trips, the Muscovy Company refused to back a third. Instead. he turned to the Dutch East India Company—direct competitors of the English—for sponsorship. Again, Hudson was instructed to sail east through the Arctic Ocean around the top of Russia. Hudson left Amsterdam on April 4, 1609

> *Hudson reached the south of Greenland on 4 June 1610. Twenty days later he sailed into the Hudson Strait at the northern end of Labrador.*

on the Dutch boat *Halve Maen* (*Half Moon* in English). When ice blocked his route east of Norway in mid-May, he turned west instead and, acting against his orders, he set sail to find a north-westerly passage around North America.

By July, Hudson had reached LaHave in Nova Scotia, where he took on supplies and made repairs. Hudson sailed south as far as Chesapeake Bay before turning back north and sailing into what is now New York Harbor. He sailed up the river that would subsequently be named after him as far as Albany before realizing it would not lead to the North-west Passage. As he explored the river, he traded furs with the local peoples. When he returned to England, he sent a report to the Dutch ambassador, which the Dutch used to stake their claim to trading rights in the region and to the fur trade.

ONE LAST TRIP

Hudson would return to North America one more time, this time under English patronage because the government had forbidden him to sail under a foreign flag. Sailing on his new ship, *Discovery*, Hudson reached the south of Greenland on

June 4, 1610. Twenty days later he sailed into the Hudson Strait at the northern end of Labrador. He thought he had finally found the North-west Passage. In front of him was a large body of water, which he named the Bay of God's Mercies (it is now known as Hudson Bay). He ordered the ship to sail down the east coast of the bay, hoping to sail south into waters that were ice-free and that would lead him to Asia.

FACT FILE

Henry Hudson

Born: ca. 1565

Disappeared: 1611

Historic Role: British explorer and navigator

Ships: *Hopewell; Halve Maen; Discovery*

Voyages: On May 1, 1607, Hudson set sail to find a north-west sea passage to Asia. In April 1908, he attempted to discover an easterly sea route to the Indies. Both voyages failed. On his final trip, Hudson miscalculated and the ship became trapped by ice

Circumstances of Death: In 1611, Hudson's crew mutinied and set him adrift. He was never heard of again

MUTINY

However, Hudson had miscalculated. By the time he realized he had found not an open strait but a huge, enclosed bay, it was too late. The weather had turned and the ship did not have time to escape from James Bay, an inlet in the south of Hudson Bay, before the ice had trapped the boat for the winter.

After enduring a freezing winter, and the ice had melted in the spring of 1611, Hudson made plans to continue exploring. However, his crew had other ideas and wanted to return home to England. The crew mutinied, forcing Hudson, his young son, and seven crew members who were either sick or loyal to Hudson, into a small boat with minimal provisions and cast them adrift.

Henry Hudson was never heard of again. Only 8 of the 13 mutinous crew of the *Discovery* returned to England to tell their tale. Although they were charged with Hudson's murder (not mutiny), they were acquitted and no one was ever punished for the crime.

Great Fire of London

A LONG HOT SUMMER, AN OVERCROWDED CITY OF TIMBER BUILDINGS AND NARROW STREETS, AN EASTERLY WIND, A SPARK, AND AN INDECISIVE LORD MAYOR WERE THE INGREDIENTS FOR A DEVASTATING FIRE THAT DESTROYED MUCH OF THE CITY OF LONDON IN 1666. WITH BETTER MANAGEMENT, THE FIRE COULD HAVE BEEN EXTINGUISHED MUCH EARLIER THAN IT WAS.

By 1666, the City of London was teeming, the densest part of what was by far the largest city in England. Bounded by Roman city walls to its north, east, and west, and by the River Thames to its south, the City was home to around 80,000 people—about one sixth of London's population. They mostly worked as small manufacturers and traders, and lived in close-set buildings. Overhanging "jetties" on the upper floors brought neighboring buildings close to one another above the notoriously narrow, traffic-choked streets.

The buildings were almost entirely made from wood—only the grandest structures were in stone or brick. Although City authorities had banned the most flammable building materials, such as thatch for roofs, no one observed the ban or bothered to enforce it. Metalworking or smithing went on in the workshops and every house had candles, ovens, and open fires.

> *The buildings were almost entirely made from wood—only the grandest structures were in stone or brick ...every house had candles, ovens, and open fires.*

A HOT, DRY SUMMER

The summer of the year 1666 had been oppressively hot. A drought had lasted since the previous November, so water supplies were low and the timber buildings were tinder-dry. Conditions were ideal for a fire to spread rapidly. Indeed, in April 1665, King Charles II had even warned the Lord Mayor of London, Sir Thomas Bloodworth, that the City was at risk, but his and other Londoners' minds were focused on a different fear. The previous year an epidemic of plague had swept through the narrow streets, killing more than 68,000 victims. Now residents were worried that the strong easterly wind might bring the plague back—in fact, it would merely fan the flames of the fire.

Soon after midnight on Sunday, September 2, in Pudding Lane, north of London Bridge, a worker at the house of the king's baker, Thomas Farynor, smelled smoke. He awoke the baker's family, who

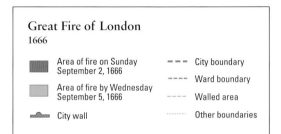

Great Fire of London
1666

- ◼ Area of fire on Sunday September 2, 1666
- ◼ Area of fire by Wednesday September 5, 1666
- 🔲 City wall
- – – – City boundary
- – – – Ward boundary
- – – – Walled area
- ·········· Other boundaries

The City of London and the extent of the Great Fire of 1666; the flames spread beyond the city walls and many feared that it would cross the river via London Bridge.

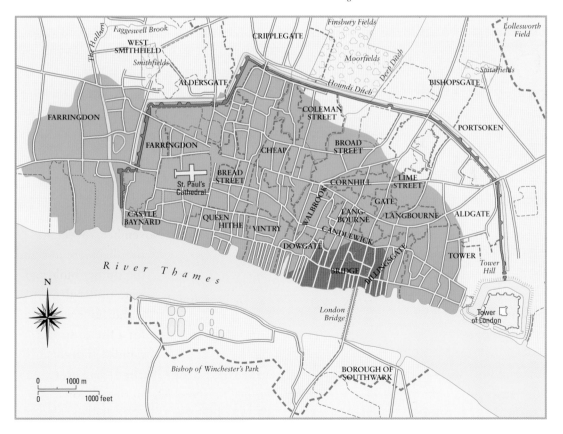

King Charles II gave orders that houses should be destroyed in order to create a firebreak and thus halt the advance of the flames. The strong winds simply fanned the flames and spread the fire farther and faster.

fled across their neighbors' roofs (a maid who was apparently too scared to leave became the first fatality of the fire). Within an hour, the fire had spread across the neighborhood, moving quickly from house to house.

Soon the blaze was sufficiently serious for Bloodworth to be woken. After considering the conflagration from his window, he is said have given his opinion that "a woman might piss it out," and returned to bed. Whatever the truth, he did nothing. And the consequences of that decision would be catastrophic for the city and its inhabitants.

CREATING FIREBREAKS

By dawn, the fire had spread to London Bridge, where a break in the buildings that then lined the bridge stopped the fire from spreading south of the river. But to the north it continued to grow. The diarist Samuel Pepys (1633–1703), who lived close to London Bridge and was both a member of parliament and an official of the English Admiralty, thought the fire sufficiently serious to inform the king and his brother, the Duke of York. Pepys took the precaution of burying his own silver in the garden in case the fire spread. Charles II ordered Pepys to instruct Bloodworth to destroy as many houses as possible, believing the fire could be contained if firebreaks were created in its path. Despite these valiant efforts, the strong winds kept fanning the fire. By the end of the Sunday, the flames had spread still farther, even traveling against the wind toward the Tower of London. By the next morning, the city was gripped by panic. The militia was called in to try to keep order as residents packed their belongings on carts or on their backs and attempted to flee down streets that were already choked with people. Chaos and panic spread while the fire advanced.

THE DEVASTATION WORSENS

Gracechurch Street, Lombard Street, and the Royal Exchange were all destroyed, but Tuesday, September 4, brought the worst destruction. The fire razed Cheapside, the widest and wealthiest street in the city. The demolition of houses had helped stop the fire from spreading east, but the flames were now making their way toward St. Paul's Cathedral. Both Newgate and Ludgate prisons were destroyed. By nightfall, St. Paul's had been burnt to the ground and molten lead from the roof flowed down Ludgate Hill.

AFTER THE SMOKE CLEARED

By Wednesday, the fire started to wane. It could not pass the brick wall of Fetter Lane and Middle Temple. The wind dropped and ongoing demolition created more firebreaks. By the time the last flames went out, some 70,000 of the city's 80,000 residents had been left homeless (although the actual official death toll was no more than a handful). Around 13,200 houses had been destroyed, along with the headquarters of the city authorities, and dozens of churches.

Although water was in short supply and there was no official fire brigade, such damage should have been avoidable. Volunteers could still take water from the Thames or Fleet rivers, forming human chains to pass along buckets of water, and once the demolition of buildings finally got underway, it proved ultimately successful. The problem was the Lord Mayor's original, ineffectual response. The local people who could have helped fight the fire fled, scared for their lives, and left the buildings to burn.

FACT FILE
Great Fire of London

Date: September 2–5, 1666

Principal Cause: Fire broke out in the house of the king's baker in Pudding Lane

Contributing Factors: Dense overcrowding, closely compacted timber buildings, high temperatures. and drought, strong easterly winds, Mayor Bloodwell's ineffectual response

Statistics: 70,000 people were left homeless; the exact death toll is unknown, but it was low

Buildings Lost: 13,200 houses, along with Gracechurch Street, Lombard Street, the Royal Exchange, Cheapside, Newgate and Ludgate prisons, the headquarters of the city authorities, St. Paul's Cathedral, and dozens of other churches

Easter Island

EASTER ISLAND IS BEST KNOWN FOR THE COLOSSAL STONE HEADS THAT LOOK OUT OVER ITS EMPTY LANDSCAPE. HOWEVER, THOSE MONUMENTS CAME AT A HUGE PRICE. ANTHROPOLOGISTS BELIEVE THEY VIRTUALLY DESTROYED THE VERY SOCIETY THAT CREATED THEM BY HASTENING DISASTROUS ECOLOGICAL CHANGE.

One of the most remote inhabited places on the planet, Easter Island is a tiny speck in the Pacific Ocean some 2,175 miles (3,500 km) off the coast of Chile and 1,240 miles (2,000 km) from its nearest inhabited neighbor. The island, more properly known now as Rapa Nui (Big Rapa), was given its popular name by Jacob Roggeveen in 1722 on Easter Sunday. It was settled quite late in the sequence of human habitation of the Polynesian islands, probably not before AD 700, and perhaps as late as 1200.

The island is formed by the peaks of three extinct volcanoes, whose crater lakes are a major source of fresh water; the island has no permanent streams or rivers. Nevertheless, the islanders, who probably arrived by canoe from one of the nearest Polynesian island groups of the Gambiers or the Marquesas, found a flourishing ecosystem with a range of trees, including palm trees that grew more than 50 feet (15 m) tall. There were flightless birds to catch for food, and plenty of fish in the surrounding waters. Their new home was tiny, little more than 15 miles (24 km) long, and no wider than 7½ miles (24 km), with a total area of 63 square miles (163.6 km square).

Over the following centuries, the island's resources were able to sustain a relatively small population that eventually reached a peak in the early 17th century...

Over the following centuries, the island's resources were able to sustain a relatively small population that eventually reached a peak in the early 17th century of some 15,000. But those resources were fragile, as was already becoming apparent, and could not withstand the stubborn persistence of the islanders' remarkable cultural beliefs.

ANCESTOR WORSHIP

Society on Rapa Nui was highly structured, based on a hierarchy of powerful chiefs and clans, and also on the worship of powerful ancestors, who were believed to watch over the living islanders, helping them. From about 1250 onward, the islanders symbolized the presence of these guardians by carving huge stone heads, called *moai*, at a quarry in the heart of the island. The tallest were more than 40 ft (12 m) high. Once carved, the heads were transported to the coast and set up on stone platforms called *ahu*, looking inland over the island with their backs to the sea. Some were erected on their own, others in groups, and some in rows. People also had smaller,

The moai *or stature heads are scattered around the perimeter of the island of Rapa Nui, all facing inward, toward land instead of the sea.*

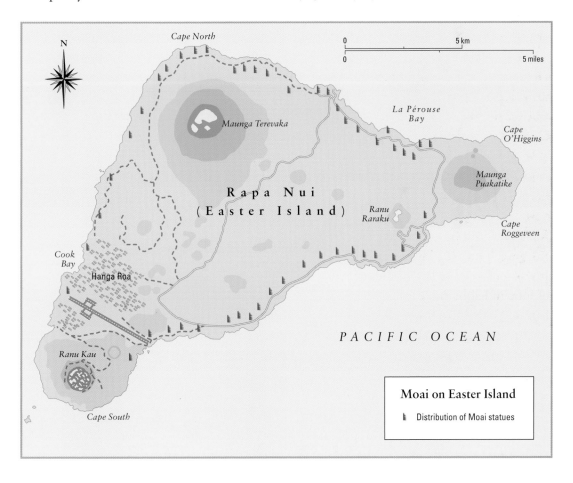

The statues of Easter Island look away from the sea, inland across a barren landscape denuded of trees. These enigmatic figures were constructed to represent the islanders' ancestors, who would watch over them.

portable versions of *moai* that they kept in their homes. These dead ancestors were thought to help provide directly for the needs of the living.

It was these great stone heads that astounded the European navigators who visited Easter Island in the early 18th century, and for which the island is still famous. About 800 survive, but by the time Europeans arrived, many had been abandoned, still in the quarry where they were being carved, while others had been toppled by raiders from other islands. The population had fallen to as low as 2,000, with the islanders living a hard and barely adequate existence. The *moai* for the most part stood gazing out over empty land.

DEFORESTATION

The collapse of the Easter Island society has become a case study of how not to harness limited resources. The main culprit seems to have been the *moai* themselves. The creation of the statues must have involved a concerted effort from virtually the whole society. Moving a 11 ton (10 tonne) piece of stone over a considerable distance needed a huge amount of manpower and a huge amount of wood. The island's tallest trees were cut down to provide rollers for transportation or to provide firewood. By around 1650, there were virtually no trees left on the island above about 10 ft (3 m)) tall. This deforestation had a catastrophic effect on the landscape. Without the protection of the trees, the poor, thin soil was more vulnerable to erosion.

Not only did the population begin to fall dramatically as life became more difficult, some anthropologists argue that the islanders turned to cannibalism.

The land birds that had lived among the trees become more scarce, and the number of sea birds also dropped. There was less wood for building, particularly fishing vessels that would have allowed the islanders to supplement their increasingly limited diet.

The islanders' commitment to creating the representations of the ancestors who were meant to improve their lives had the opposite effect. What's more, the efforts required for construction meant that they paid less attention than they might to developing farming or otherwise finding alternative ways to survive.

AN ISLAND IN DECLINE

The ecological collapse was accompanied by social upheaval. Not only did the population begin to fall dramatically as life became more difficult, some anthropologists argue that the islanders turned to cannibalism. The old hierarchy, based on the worship of the dead through the statues and the rule of their living heirs, gave way to new forms of connecting with the ancestors. The power of the *moai* had waned. Easter Island society did not vanish altogether, although it came close. Roggeveen visited in 1722, Spanish explorers came in 1770, and four years later, Captain James Cook visited the island. But after another ship visited in the 1820s, the islanders had become so hostile to visitors and the island so riven by internal wars, that no one visited again until the 1860s.

At this point, the poor islanders were captured in their hundreds by Peruvian slave traders, while many others fell victim to epidemics of smallpox and tuberculosis, probably brought to the island by outsiders. In 1877, at its lowest point, the island's population was only 111. By that time, there were more *moai* than there were humans to watch over.

Salem Witch Trials

IN ONE OF THE STRANGEST INCIDENTS IN THE HISTORY OF COLONIAL AMERICA, THE UNDISTINGUISHED VILLAGE OF SALEM SAW AN OUTBREAK OF COLLECTIVE HYSTERIA THAT LED TO 100 VILLAGERS BEING ACCUSED OF WITCHCRAFT AND 19 PEOPLE BEING EXECUTED BEFORE THE WITCH MANIA PASSED AS QUICKLY AS IT HAD BEGUN.

Witch trials were nothing new in Christian history. Followers of strict forms of the Protestant faith, such as the Puritanism that dominated Massachusetts, were constantly on the alert for signs of satanic possession. What made the Salem outbreak so different was that it came quite late in the history of witchcraft—witch trials had been declining in Europe for some time— and it occurred in the 'New World', where it soon involved the whole of the colonial administration.

THE FIRST VISIONS

The mania began in February 1692, when Abigail Williams and Elizabeth Parris, niece and daughter respectively of the village minister Samuel Parris, began to suffer fits. Their bodies contorted and they went temporarily blind, deaf, and dumb, after which they claimed to have seen visions of witches' spirits. They accused a slave girl Tituba, and two respectable widows, Sarah Osburn and Sarah Good, of leaving their bodies to do evil. Soon the seizures spread among other young women in the village, and so did the spectral evidence against the so-called witches. By the end of May, the village jail held 39 accused witches.

On June 2, 1692, the new governor of Massachusetts, William Phips, appointed a special court of seven judges to try the accused. In a series of dramatic court appearances, the accused came face to face with the accusers who claimed to have seen them walking the town at night in the shape of specters. Whatever denials the accused made were taken only as a proof of Satan's deviousness. Some tried to save themselves by "confessing" to their crimes—and implicating others

The Salem witch trials took place in Massachusetts, a most unlikely place to give rise to witchcraft and mass hysteria.

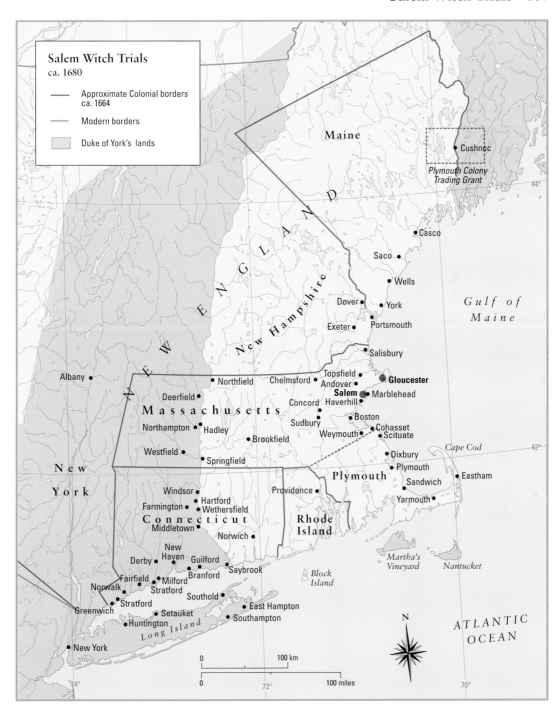

Salem Witch Trials
ca. 1680

——— Approximate Colonial borders
       ca. 1664

——— Modern borders

        Duke of York's lands

Maine

Cushnoc

*Plymouth Colony
Trading Grant*

N E W   E N G L A N D

Casco

Saco

Wells

Dover

York

Exeter

Portsmouth

*Gulf of
Maine*

New Hampshire

Salisbury

Albany

Northfield

Chelmsford

Topsfield

Andover

Gloucester

Deerfield

Concord

Salem

Marblehead

Haverhill

M a s s a c h u s e t t s

Northampton

Hadley

Sudbury

Boston

Brookfield

Weymouth

Cohasset

Scituate

Westfield

Springfield

Dixbury

Plymouth

Cape Cod

New
York

Windsor

Hartford

Providence

Plymouth

Sandwich

Eastham

Farmington

Wethersfield

Yarmouth

C o n n e c t i c u t

Middletown

Norwich

Rhode
Island

New
Haven

Derby

Guilford

Saybrook

*Block
Island*

*Martha's
Vineyard*

Nantucket

Fairfield

Branford

Milford

Stratford

Southold

Norwalk

Stratford

Southold

Setauket

East Hampton

Greenwich

Huntington

Southampton

Long Island

New York

N

ATLANTIC
OCEAN

0   100 km

0   100 miles

Historic home of Judge Corwin, one of the judges who took part in the trials. It is now the only standing structure with ties to the Salem witch trials of 1692.

This time, no one spoke in her defense and she was hanged on June 10, 1692, on Gallows Hill.

HYSTERIA TAKES HOLD

The next group of five women found guilty and sentenced to death, however, included a woman named Rebecca Nurse, who was widely admired for her piety and for helping others. Not even the magistrate in the trial, John Hathorne, thought she was guilty (Hathorne's own sister spoke in Nurse's defense). But when the jury acquitted Nurse, the afflicted women behind the accusations flew into more seizures, swearing again that they had seen her spirit leave her body. The jury changed its verdict. When William Phips then reprieved Nurse, another outbreak of seizures forced him to withdraw his reprieve. On July 19, Nurse was hanged with her four companions.

As the trials went on, however, so the influence of the accusers began to wane. The people they targeted were now respected pillars of society, who spoke out to defend themselves and defied the tyranny by pleading not guilty. Unease began to grow. Then Giles Corey, an 80-year-old farmer whose wife had already been executed, declined to recognize the

who they said had joined them in the devil's work. Soon accusations had spread from Salem to include the neighboring villages of Andover, Gloucester, Haverhill, and Topsfield. Meanwhile, two of Massachusetts' leading clerics, the Boston ministers Increase and Cotton Mather, could see the dangers. They advised Governor Phips to proceed with caution. But the trials were run by civil instead of religious authorities, and they forged ahead with horrible consequences.

Initially, many of the accused came from among the very poor or those who lived on society's margins. They included Bridget Bishop, who had already been tried for witchcraft in 1680. In that trial, she had been freed after a plea from her pastor.

court or to enter a plea. That protected his legacy to his heirs, because if he were convicted of witchcraft he would have his property taken from him, but it left him open to be tortured until he made a plea, or died. On September 19, Corey was pressed to death beneath a pile of stones. By now, twenty people had been executed for witchcraft, while dozens more languished in jail as they awaited trial.

THE BUBBLE BURSTS
With their veracity coming into doubt, the afflicted grew wilder in their accusations. They accused prominent members of society, including the wife of Governor Phips himself. Enough was enough. Even the priest Samuel Parris, whose daughter and niece led the accusations, and who had been one of the most ardent witch-hunters, now began to doubt the wisdom of the trials. Early in October, Increase Mather condemned the trials in Salem and openly questioned the reliability of spectral evidence. On October 12, Phips forbade any further arrests and at the end of the month he dissolved the court. A new court staged two more trials—Phips reprieved the three people found guilty—and the remaining accused were released from jail

in May the following year on Phips' order, once they had paid for the cost of their time in jail.

The hysteria had ended. Quite what had caused it, however, remains a mystery, although some believe it began out of family feuds, spite, and attention-seeking. Many theories allude to the strict Puritan tradition in which Satan was a direct and real presence in everyday life. Others highlight the prominent role in the accusations of pubescent young women who were undergoing profound physical and emotional changes, suggesting they were perhaps more vulnerable to seizures and delusions. But once the witch mania took hold—encouraged by the participation of the Colonial administration—the trials became a way first to persecute the widows, spinsters, and old men who lived on edge of society, and then for the accusers to strike at those higher than themselves on the social scale. It remains a difficult and somewhat shameful episode in American colonial history.

> *Increase Mather condemned the trials in Salem and openly questioned the reliability of spectral evidence ... Phips forbade further arrests and dissolved the court.*

Scilly Naval Disaster

LEADING THE PRIDE OF THE WORLD'S STRONGEST MARITIME FLEET, THE ROYAL NAVY, BACK TO THE ENGLISH CHANNEL AFTER AN EXPEDITION TO THE MEDITERRANEAN, SIR CLOUDESLEY SHOVELL MANAGED TO RUN OVER ONE-QUARTER OF HIS SHIPS AGROUND ON THE ROCKY SCILLY ISLES. FOUR VESSELS SANK AND UP TO 2,000 SAILORS LOST THEIR LIVES, INCLUDING SHOVELL HIMSELF.

During the summer of 1707, Sir Cloudesley led a fleet of British ships to fight the French in the War of the Spanish Succession. The British fleet sailed to the Mediterranean, where it joined Austrian and Dutch ships besieging the French port of Toulon. The combined forces attacked the port, but despite inflicting some damage on the French fleet, were unable to defeat it. Ultimately, the Franco-Spanish alliance proved too strong for their enemies and the British were ordered to return home.

BLOWN OFF COURSE

The fleet of 21 ships sailed from Gibraltar bound for Portsmouth in late October 1707, with Sir Cloudesley on board his flagship HMS *Association*. The journey was extremely rough, with bad storms and gales as the ships crossed the turbulent waters of the Bay of Biscay. When the fleet sailed out into the Atlantic on its way to England, the weather worsened, with storms pushing the ships farther off their planned course.

In the early 18th century, sailors worked out their latitude—their position north or south on the surface of the Earth—by observing the position of the sun and other heavenly bodies. But they could only calculate their longitude—their position east or west—according to their speed and directions from previous readings. This process involved a certain amount of estimation, because it relied on exact timings, and no clock then existed that could keep accurate time on board a ship on rough seas.

> *Sir Cloudesley charted his fleet's position by astronomical observation and by consultation with the sailing masters of his other ships. They all agreed ...*

Sir Cloudesley Shovell, the commander of the British naval fleet that ran aground on the Scilly Isles.

Sir Cloudesley charted his fleet's position by astronomical observation and by consultation with the sailing masters of his other ships. They all agreed with Sir Cloudesley that they were west of Ushant, on the north-west tip of France. The only dissenting voice was the sailing master of HMS *Lenox* who argued that the fleet was close to the Scilly Isles. and that three hours' sailing would bring the islands within sight and, of course, would then pose a threat to the fleet. Sir Cloudesley went with the majority view and charted the course as if the fleet was off the French coast. Unfortunately, the sailing master of the *Lenox* was proved right.

FOUR SHIPS DOWN

On the night of October 22, 1707, the fleet entered the mouth of the English Channel. It was indeed dangerously close to the Scilly Isles, and in appalling weather conditions, too. Before the navigational mistake could be rectified, the fleet struck the rocks. Within a very short time, four ships were lost: HMS *Association*, HMS *Eagle*, HMS *Romney*, and HMS *Firebrand*.

Sir Cloudesley's flagship, HMS *Association*, was the first ship to founder. It struck the Outer Gilstone Rock at 8:00 p.m., and sank with the loss of its entire crew of 800 seamen, including the Admiral of the Fleet himself. Sailing closely behind were the *St. George* and HMS *Phoenix*. The *St. George* hit rocks but managed to stay afloat, while the *Phoenix* ran aground but remained seaworthy.

HMS *Eagle* hit the Crim Rocks and sank with the loss of its entire crew of between 200 and 300 seamen commanded by Captain Robert Hancock. HMS *Romney*, a smaller ship commanded by Captain William Coney, hit Bishop Rock and sank with just one survivor, the quartermaster George Lawrence. The final loss was the fireship, HMS *Firebrand*. Under the command of Captain Francis Percy, the ship hit the Outer Gilstone Rock. Although it survived the initial impact on the rocks, the vessel later foundered in Smith Sound with the loss of 28 of its 40-man crew.

The precise number of men who died in the disaster has never been finally established. Many bodies were washed up on the shores of the islands, including Sir Cloudesley Shovell's body that came ashore at Porthellick Cove, where a monument now stands to him.

THE LONGITUDE ACT

The Scilly naval disaster was one of the British Navy's worst maritime calamities. Its impact was made worse because it happened in home waters and during peacetime. It led to calls for more reliable forms of navigation and for the invention of more reliable navigational aids. The Longitude Act of 1714 established a Board of Longitude, which offered a large financial reward (£20,000) for anyone who could devise an accurate method of establishing longitude at sea. The prize was

A historical engraving illustrating the Scilly Naval disaster in which some 2,000 British seamen lost their lives.

Rocky outcrops and the rough shoreline of the Scillys continue to be unforgiving of navigational mistakes.

finally claimed in 1773, when self-taught clockmaker John Harrison invented the marine chronometer, which was the key to solving the problem of accurately working out longitude at sea. Harrison's struggle to invent such a chronometer and his ultimate success has been vividly recounted by Dava Sobel in her book *Longitude*.

More recent examination of the causes of the disaster suggests that uncertainty in measuring longitude was not the only problem. It seems likely that the sailing masters also did not have the fleet's correct latitude, and that the position of the Scilly Isles was not precisely charted on the contemporary maps of the time. The task facing Sir Cloudesley and his sailing masters was almost impossible.

American Independence

ABOUT 150 YEARS AFTER THE FIRST BRITISH COLONY WAS ESTABLISHED IN NORTH AMERICA IN 1607, COLONIAL AMERICANS BEGAN TO WONDER IF THEY WOULD BE BETTER OFF GOVERNING THEMSELVES. THE BRITISH HAD AMPLE OPPORTUNITIES TO ADDRESS THEIR GRIEVANCES, BUT INSTEAD ADOPTED A BULLISH, HEAVY-HANDED ATTITUDE THAT PROVOKED AN UNWINNABLE WAR.

Colonial Americans were governed from London, with governors of each colony appointed by the British government. Most importantly, the colonies were subject to British taxes—but they didn't have any say in how those taxes were spent. There were no colonial members of parliament to speak up for the colonies when it came to debating how to distribute the money. That situation irritated an increasing number of colonists.

Things began to come to a head in the 1760s. Leading Americans, such as Samuel Adams of Boston and Patrick Henry of Virginia, had already begun to object to being governed by the British. The colonies had become prosperous; many people lived there, and cities, such as Philadelphia, were thriving centers of trade. But the British government, without consultation, began to pass a series of laws to raise taxes that infuriated the colonial Americans.

First they taxed trade with the West Indies, another British colony. Anything traded between the Thirteen Colonies and the West Indies, which were just next door in the Caribbean, had to be carried in British ships—and taxes paid to London. The Stamp Tax raised money by charging for an official stamp that had to be added to legal documents, newspapers, and even playing cards. American protests began to become more strident, gathered under the simple slogan: "no taxation without representation." Tempers ran high. In Boston, British soldiers shot dead five Colonial civilians who were protesting against the British military presence in the so-called Boston Massacre of March 1770.

For one group of Bostonians, the last straw was a tax on imported tea. The

The map opposite shows the extent of the territory controlled by the British crown at the beginning of the War of Independence.

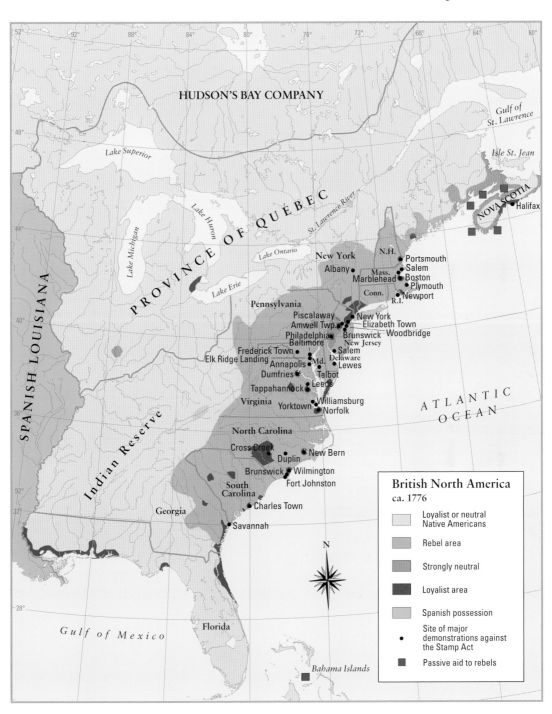

HUDSON'S BAY COMPANY

Gulf of
St. Lawrence

Lake Superior

Isle St. Jean

NOVA SCOTIA

Halifax

Lake Huron

PROVINCE OF QUÉBEC

St. Lawrence River

Lake Michigan

Lake Ontario

Lake Erie

New York

N.H.

Portsmouth
Salem
Boston
Plymouth
Newport

Albany

Mass.
Marblehead

Conn.

R.I.

SPANISH LOUISIANA

Pennsylvania

Piscalaway
Amwell Twp.
Philadelphia
Baltimore
Frederick Town
Elk Ridge Landing
Annapolis
Dumfries
Tappahannock
Virginia
Yorktown

New York
Elizabeth Town
Brunswick
New Jersey
Salem
Delaware
Lewes
Talbot
Leeds
Williamsburg
Norfolk

Woodbridge

Md.

ATLANTIC
OCEAN

Indian Reserve

North Carolina

Cross Creek
Duplin
Brunswick
South
Carolina

New Bern
Wilmington
Fort Johnston

Georgia

Charles Town

Savannah

Gulf of Mexico

Florida

Bahama Islands

British North America
ca. 1776

Loyalist or neutral
Native Americans

Rebel area

Strongly neutral

Loyalist area

Spanish possession

• Site of major
demonstrations against
the Stamp Act

■ Passive aid to rebels

British allowed tea to be imported to America only from the East Indies on British ships, and the trade was tightly controled by the British East India Company. Again, the tea was heavily taxed by the British, although tax on tea imported into Britain was being cut at exactly the same time. Some politicians warned King George III about overtaxing the colonies, but the government ignored them. The country was heavily in debt after the war against France for the control of Canada in the 1750s, and the government needed the tax revenue to settle its debts and to pay the salaries of officials in the colonies. The king—he of *The Madness of King George* fame—resolutely stuck to his right to treat North America as a subject power, despite widespread warnings that doing so would lead to huge problems in the colonies.

THE BOSTON "TEA PARTY"

In October 1773, ships carrying tea docked in Boston Harbor. The governor refused to pay the tax, but also refused to let the boats return to Britain. On the night of December 16, a gang of colonials went on board the ships and dumped all the tea—342 chests—into Boston Harbor. Some were dressed as Mohawk Native Americans, but the disguise didn't fool anyone. The British response was predictable—but no more effective for that. They introduced what became known to Americans as the "Intolerable Acts." They closed Boston Harbor to shipping and brought the colony of Massachusetts under direct royal government. If the measures were intended to squash any signs of rebellion, they had the opposite effect. British troops began to search for weapons stored by the Americans. On the night of April 18, 1775, troops set out to march from Boston to seize an arsenal maintained by the colonial militia at Concord. Alerted by the famous midnight ride of Boston silversmith Paul Revere, the militia was ready to stop them. At first light on April 19, shots were fired when the two sides clashed at Lexington Green, just outside Concord. With those shots, the American Revolution had begun.

All was not lost for the British. Many Americans had no desire to leave Britain's empire. Indeed, the majority of the text of the Declaration of Independence, as drafted by Thomas Jefferson in 1776, was a list of grievances against the British monarch that might still have been addressed. However, King George refused to treat the protests as anything more than a rebellion against the rule of law. Despite plenty of voices in parliament advising moderation, the British government wouldn't acknowledge the legitimacy of the forces arrayed against them nor their argument. Instead, the government decided that it could silence the resentment by going to war.

It was a fateful decision. British troops would be fighting in hostile territory on the far side of the Atlantic, where it would be difficult to supply and reinforce, against an enemy that could draw on local knowledge and large reserves of manpower (and the support of the meddling French, who were always eager to weaken British influence overseas). Even though one-third of Americans remained loyal to the British —they were known as Loyalists or King's Men—the cause was doomed.

VICTORY FOR THE "PATRIOTS"

The Americans facing the British dubbed themselves "Patriots.' On paper, they stood little chance against the might of the British army, but with training from George Washington and his Prussian chief of staff, Baron Friedrich Wilhelm von Steuben, the Continental rmy improved greatly over the first two years of the war. A colonial victory at Saratoga in 1777 split the British forces in North America, and led inevitably to the decisive victory at Yorktown, Virginia, on October 19, 1781. Trapped on a peninsula against the Atlantic, with French ships blockading any hope of reinforcement or escape,

Lord Cornwallis had little choice but to surrender. It was said that at the formal ceremony, a British band played a well-known tune with a peculiarly apt title, 'The World Turned Upside Down', highlighting the end of British influence after nearly 175 years. Britain continued to hold sway in Canada for another century; however, Canada gained its independence through peaceful means.

FACT FILE
American Independence

Leading Figures: George Washington, Baron Friedrich Wilhelm von Steuben (USA); King George III of England

Major Issues: American colonies were subject to British taxes and had no say in how they were spent

Major Incidents: Boston Massacre (1770); Boston Tea Party (1773); Intolerable Acts (1774); the battle at Lexington Green (1775); Declaration of Independence (1776); colonial victory at Saratoga (1777)

British Mistake: Declaration of Independence contained grievances that might still have been addressed by King George, but he refused to treat the protests as anything more than rebellion

Key Event: Battle of Yorktown (October 19, 1781) spelled the end for Britain in the War of Independence

Nineteenth Century

This century was no different from any preceeding age when it came to disasters and mistakes. There were many military decisions that resulted in disaster, but perhaps Napoleon's winter campaign in Russia is remarkable for the humiliation it inflicted on Napoleon and on France. The Charge of the Light Brigade is often seen as heroic, but it was also a disaster for those involved. The cultural fallout for Native Americans from the battles of Little Big Horn and of Wounded Knee has been profound. It was not all military disaster though; pollution and fire were at the root of the Great Stink and the Great Chicago Fire, while an ill-conceived commercial decision cost Western Union millions when it failed to grab the telephone when the invention was offered to the company.

Napoleon in Russia

IN JUNE 1812, NAPOLEON LED UP TO 610,000 MEN ACROSS THE NIEMAN RIVER INTO RUSSIA. BY THE TIME HE RETURNED SIX MONTHS LATER, FEWER THAN 100,000 MEN REMAINED ALIVE. HISTORY'S GREATEST GENERAL HAD LOST ONE OF HISTORY'S GREATEST ARMIES IN A GESTURE OF REMARKABLE AMBITION AND FOLLY.

By 1807, Napoleon had created a French empire that stretched from Spain to the historical border between Lithuania and Poland, the Nieman river. He had met with the Russian Czar Alexander I on a raft moored on the river to agree a peace treaty that left Napoleon in charge of western Europe. Only Britain resisted his rule, and Napoleon had ambitions to blockade European trade with Britain in order to force its economic collapse and leave it open to invasion.

But Britain's Royal Navy kept the blockade from being effective and soon various of Napoleon's partners began to break it: first Portugal, where the British joined the Portuguese to fight the Peninsular War against Napoleon from 1808; then Sweden, which Napoleon also invaded in 1808. Now, in 1812, Russia also began trading with Britain. Napoleon was eager to punish the csar and bring him back onboard. Using an alleged threat from Russia on Poland as an excuse, Napoleon planned to march on Moscow, Russia's emotional and cultural capital, and also destroy the political capital St. Petersburg.

These scorched-earth tactics meant that the leading French units found it difficult to find enough to live on. By the time the rear of the army arrived, there was nothing left.

The *Grand Armée* he had assembled for the task was the largest fighting force that had ever been raised in Europe at that time, comprising somewhere between 440,000 and 610,000 men from France and its various allies. It faced vast numbers of Russian defenders; roughly 488,000 men were mobilized and positioned deep within their country.

THE RUSSIANS FALL BACK

The invading army met little military resistance as it crossed the Nieman into what was known as Russian Poland. Its main obstacles were the unpaved lanes, the difficulty of supply lines keeping up with the advance, and the weather that changed rapidly from baking heat to thunderstorms that turned the ground to mud. As the French marched on to Vilnius and beyond, the Russian forces fell back, destroying anything that might be useful to the invaders. These scorched-earth tactics meant that the leading French units found it difficult to find enough to live on. By the time the rear of the army arrived, there was nothing left. The French were suffering from lack of supplies, and as a consequence, desertion, starvation, and disease—mainly typhus—cost the *Grand Armée* up to one-fifth of its men in just the opening weeks of the campaign.

Eventually, Tsar Alexander I decided to replace Prince Pyotr Bagration as Russian commander and appoint Mikhail Illarionovich Kutusov to stiffen the Russian defense. To begin with, Kutusov was no more anxious than his predecessor to give battle, apart from a clash at Smolensk. Finally, in September, he found a defensive position where he was willing to fight, at Borodino, not far outside Moscow. The battle of Borodino turned out to be the largest clash of the entire campaign.

One-quarter of a million men clashed, and both sides suffered huge casualties. At the end of the day, Napoleon's troops controlled the battlefield—the traditional criterion of victory—and yet while the Russians were greatly weakened, they were not defeated. Napoleon's men were too exhausted to pursue and defeat their enemy. The Russians fell back, leaving the way to Moscow open.

Napoleon marched into Moscow on September 14, 1812, expecting the city to capitulate—only to find there was no one left to surrender. Kutusov had ordered the city evacuated and its stores destroyed. The governor Feodore Rostopchin and the civil authorities were nowhere to be seen. The Russians would not fight and they would not surrender. It was a breach of the "rules" of warfare, and it put Napoleon in an impossible position. With no Russian authorities to help impose order on the occupation, his soldiers ran amok, looting what they could find. That same evening fires broke out among the wooden buildings. Within days, more than 80 percent of the city had burnt down, removing whatever makeshift accommodation the French had found. With no supplies to be found and nowhere for his troops to stay, Napoleon had no choice. After only a month in Moscow, he ordered the retreat.

FORCED BACK TO FRANCE

The French were in an unenviable position, hundreds of miles from friendly territory, facing a Russian force that had been reinforced since Borodino, and with the winter closing in. Their return was harried by Kutusov, who aimed to force them back over much the same ground they had already crossed, which a combination of Russian scorched-earth tactics and French foraging had devastated. Indeed, there was not even grass for the French cavalry, who killed their horses for food and continued the march on foot.

Artillery and supply wagons were abandoned while men starved, fell back. or deserted. The stragglers and deserters fell into the hands of the Russian forces that shadowed the retreat, mainly bands of Cossack horsemen who either killed them, or stripped them of all useful clothing and abandoned them, or even sold them to peasants.

There were a number of battles along the retreat, as Kutusov forced Napoleon to stick to the barren route home, but worse came as the *Grand Armée* crossed the Berezina river in Belarus on November 26, 1812. Napoleon had intended to walk across the frozen river on the ice, but it had thawed. His engineers had to construct two 330 ft (100 m) bridges so the French could escape being trapped between two advancing Russian armies. But the French rearguard, unable to reach the bridges, lost up to 20,000 soldiers plus an unknown number of camp followers—between 30,000 and 40,000 people died in all.

The *Grand Armée* faced two more weeks of purgatory before it left Russian territory

on December 14, 1812. It was said that only 93,000 of the 440,000 soldiers who had set out managed to survive and return to French soil—although accurate numbers are impossible to establish. By then, the emperor himself had abandoned his men and hastened to Paris to deal with an attempted coup d'état. His shattered troops were left to find their own ways home and Napoleon's Russian campaign became a byword for military failure.

Napoleon's route across Europe and into Russia makes it clear how closely he was compelled to follow his advance route when in retreat.

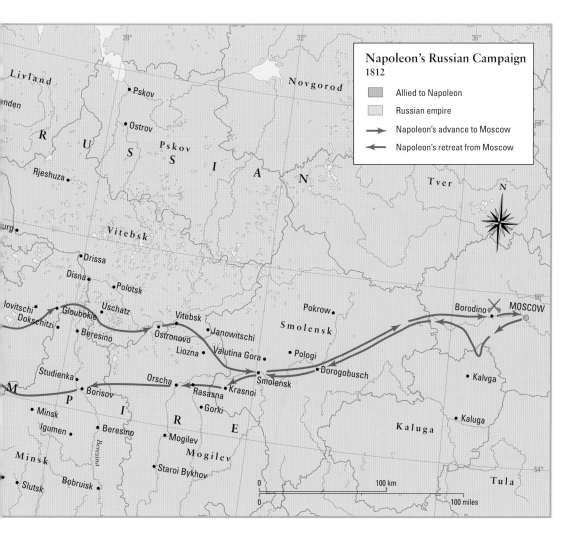

Charge of the Light Brigade

BRITISH POET LAUREATE ALFRED LORD TENNYSON PUBLISHED A POEM ABOUT A RECENT MILITARY DISASTER. IT BECAME FAMOUS FOR ITS REFRAIN "INTO THE VALLEY OF DEATH RODE THE SIX HUNDRED." AS TENNYSON MADE CLEAR, THE DISASTER WAS THE RESULT OF MISTAKES, PERSONALITY CLASHES, AND STUBBORNNESS AT THE TOP OF THE BRITISH ARMY: SOMEONE HAD BLUNDERED.

The British were brought to the Crimea Peninsula on the Black Sea in the mid-19th century by concerns over what would become of the declining Turkish Ottoman empire, or the "Eastern Question," as it was known. The vast Russian empire, which bordered Ottoman territory, had ambitions to seize Turkish land. In May 1853, Czar Nicholas I occupied the Ottoman provinces on the Danube and in retaliation the Ottomans declared war on Russia. They were soon joined by the British and the French who, despite being reluctant to go to war, were suspicious of and worried about the tsar's territorial and imperial ambitions.

At the second line of defense, the Russian cavalry was turned back by the Scottish 93rd Highland Regiment, arrayed in two long rows ... the Thin Red Line.

THE THIN RED LINE

British and French armies sailed through the Dardanelles into the Black Sea, where they besieged Sevastopol, the base of Russia's Black Sea Fleet. Shortly afterward, in an attempt to relieve the siege, some 25,000 Russian troops attacked the allied supply base at Balaclava. The Battle of Balaclava began at 6:00 a.m. on October 25, 1853, with a Russian artillery bombardment that drove the defenders from the redoubts, or fortified positions, which formed the first line of defense. But at the second line of defense, the Russian cavalry was turned back by the Scottish 93rd Highland Regiment, arrayed in two long rows that became famously known as the "Thin Red Line."

Now, the British overall commander Lord Raglan, watching the battle from high ground, sent in the cavalry, the pride of the British army led by the cream of the aristocracy. Raglan ordered the Heavy Brigade to charge a far larger Russian cavalry force, only to be frustrated when the Light Brigade failed to join the fight to win a decisive victory. The Light Brigade's commander Lord Cardigan believed that he had been ordered to defend his position, not to use his initiative. However, part of Cardigan's reluctance to move was pique; the order had come from his brother-in-law Lord Lucan, the commander of the British cavalry, whom Cardigan detested just as much as Lucan detested him.

CONFUSION OVER "THE GUNS"

Raglan wanted the cavalry to prevent the Russians from carrying off British guns

Strategic positions of all the major players on the fateful day make it clear just how disastrous the charge was.

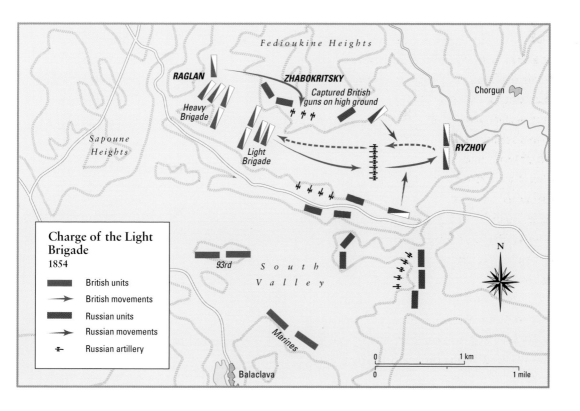

This historic engraving from 1857, only a few years after the conflict, shows the taking of Malakoff by the French army. It also makes clear just how bloody the Crimean war was.

they had captured from the redoubts on high ground between the two valleys of the battlefield. But from the valley where Lucan and Cardigan waited with their horsemen, neither the Russians nor the guns were visible. They did not move. Exasperated, Raglan dictated another order: "10:45. Lord Raglan wants the cavalry to advance rapidly to the front— follow the enemy and try to prevent the enemy carrying away the guns—Troop Horse Artillery may accompany—French cavalry is on your left." Raglan shouted after the messenger, Captain Louis Nolan, "Tell Lord Lucan the cavalry is to attack immediately."

Lucan did not understand what guns the order referred to. Again, he hesitated, much to the annoyance of the messenger Captain Nolan, who was aware of Raglan's frustration on the heights. "Attack, sir!" urged Nolan. Still perplexed, Lucan responded, "Attack what? What guns, sir?" Nolan replied, "There, my lord, is your enemy! There are your guns!"

Nolan gestured broadly to the east—but instead of indicating the guns being moved on the heights, he seemed to be pointing to a Russian battery set up at the far end of the valley.

The order was pure suicide, but Lucan passed it to Cardigan. Cardigan protested, "There is a battery in front, a battery on each flank, and the ground is covered with Russian riflemen." Had the two men been on better terms with one another, there might have been time to clarify Raglan's precise meaning. Instead Lucan insisted, "Lord Raglan will have it. We have no choice but to obey." Lucan would lead the Heavy Brigade behind the Light Brigade.

Arranging his men in two lines, Cardigan began his advance. The observers on the heights waited for him to turn toward the heights, but the Light Brigade held its course as it gathered speed. Now the Russian guns on the flanks started firing. The first British casualty was Captain Nolan, who had rushed to the front of the charge when a shell burst next to him. There is some suggestion that Nolan had realized at this point that Cardigan was going the wrong way and was trying to halt him.

Halfway down the 1¼ mile (2 km) long valley, the Russian guns ahead opened up. Under fire from three sides, the surviving horsemen charged the guns, hacking their way through the line and into the rear. The Russians began to fall back. An unlikely British triumph was on the cards—but the Light Brigade was on its own. Lucan had halted his Heavy Brigade, commenting bitterly, "They have sacrificed the Light Brigade; they shall not have the Heavy, if I can help it." The Russians, seeing that the horsemen were isolated, rallied their retreating men and drove the trapped Light Brigade back.

CE N'EST PAS LA GUERRE

Around 673 men had begun the charge. Only 195 made it back to the lines with their horses. In little more than 20 minutes, 118 men had been killed, 127 wounded, and some 60 taken prisoner. But who was to blame? The answer for the British public was Lord Lucan, who was condemned for not interpreting Raglan's order correctly, nor using his initiative although he argued that Raglan did not encourage him to use his initiative in any circumstance. Cardigan, on the other hand, returned home a hero. The best remembered verdict on the whole incident, apart from Tennyson's poem, is a quote from one of the watching observers, the French Marshal Pierre Bosquet: "*C'est magnifique, mais ce n'est pas la guerre, c'est de la folie.*" ("It is magnificent but it is not war, it is madness.")

The Great Stink

IN THE MID-NINETEENTH CENTURY, BRITAIN WAS THE WORLD'S LEADING POWER.
QUEEN VICTORIA'S EMPIRE STRETCHED AROUND THE WORLD AND THE ROYAL NAVY
RULED THE WAVES. THE HOUSES OF PARLIAMENT IN LONDON HAD AN ORNATE NEW
HOME, BUT IN **1858**, PARLIAMENT AND THE REST OF THE CITY WERE BROUGHT TO A
HALT BY A NOXIOUS SMELL SO BAD IT BECAME KNOWN AS "THE GREAT STINK."

The smell of human excrement was the problem. In the unusually hot summer of 1858, raw sewage clogged the city's sewers and flowed untreated into the Thames, which became an open latrine. The stench was so appalling that parliament had to cover its windows in curtains coated with chloride of lime. Worse still, cholera was rife throughout the city.

The problem was compounded by the sheer size of London. Its infrastructure could not cope with its huge and rapidly growing population.

FLUSHING OUT THE PROBLEM

One major cause of the problem lay, ironically, in the new sanitary devices intended to remove the issue of sewage from daily life. The recent invention of the flush toilet had enabled many Londoners to abandon their chamber pots. But while the water closet represented a step forward, the water and waste went directly into existing cesspits, which some 200,000 London homes had directly beneath their floorboards. Unable or unwilling to pay to have their cesspits emptied, many households simply left them to overflow into the streets; the waste found its way into drains designed only to carry away rainwater. Even the smartest houses stank of human waste. Londoners simply learnt to live with the smell.

The problem was compounded by the sheer size of London. Its infrastructure could not cope with its huge and rapidly growing population. It was by far the largest city in a country where the 1851 census revealed that more than half the population now lived in towns and cities. The problem of waste removal was more acute in London simply because of its large size. With a birth rate that had been rising for 70 years, a shortage of housing, and limited rural employment, more and more people crowded into London. Even outside its notorious slums, such as Seven Dials, the streets were overcrowded, filthy, and unhealthy. Summer diarrhea was common and water-borne diseases, such as cholera became a real concern.

The Houses of Parliament sit on the Thames and were affected by "the Great Stink." Members of Parliament were finally moved to do something about the problem when the smell stopped the daily work of government.

LACK OF INVESTMENT

Local authorities were, in theory, responsible for running London and its parishes, but most Londoners resented paying taxes. They tended to vote for the cheapest government they could. Elected councillors thus promised and delivered nothing like an adequate kind of infrastructure. The net result was too little investment in sewers, street paving and cleaning, clean wate, and proper housing.

The smell was not the only problem. Potentially fatal cholera arrived in London

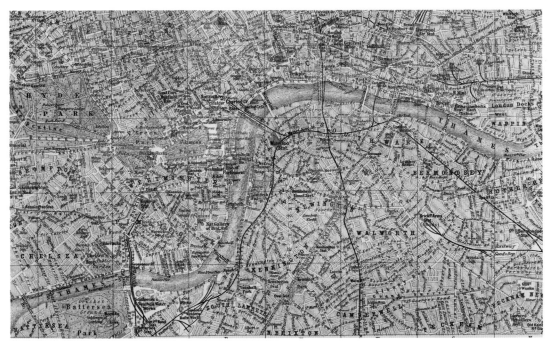

This nineteenth-century map of London shows the course of the Thames as it snakes its way through the metropolis.

from Asia in the early 1830s. It became widespread during the 1840s, largely because people mistakenly believed cholera was spread through the air, so took inadequate precautions against it. (It was only in 1854 that Dr, John Snow discovered that cholera was spread by contaminated water after studying an outbreak in Soho in central London.)

A cholera outbreak in 1847 forced the government to pass the 1848 Public Health Act, which established local boards of health to take responsibility for sewers, ensuring a clean water supply, and regulating slaughterhouses. In practice, they did little, and the General Board of Health was soon abolished.

In the summer of 1858, all these negative elements coalesced into a perfect storm. The inadequate sewage system, the lack of investment in the infrastructure, and the steaming hot weather made London a horrible, dangerous, and smelly place to live for its two million inhabitants.

Diseases were rife, mainly cholera and typhoid. The hot weather encouraged bacteria to thrive in the filthy water of the Thames, which for years had received sewage directly from the small tributaries that crossed the city. Now the Thames backed up; at high tide, a river of ordure threatened to overflow the streets. Terrified Londoners fled the city while wealthy residents soaked their curtains in perfume to try to mask the smell. Likewise, members of parliament in the Houses of Parliament soaked the curtains in chloride of lime to block the noxious smells wafting in from the sewage-laden river below.

A NEW SEWERAGE SYSTEM

The crisis came to an end only when heavy rains arrived to flush out the drains and the rivers. By then, Parliament had been forced to act. Ignoring suggestions, such as turning the tower of the Houses of Parliament into a chimney for burning the noxious waste, or carting human excrement into the countryside outside the city to be used as manure, MPs rushed through an act ordering the construction of a proper underground sewerage system.

In 1859, Joseph Bazalgette, the chief engineer of the newly created Metropolitan Board of Works, came up with a masterly scheme: some 2,200 miles (3,600 km) of underground and street sewers to intercept sewage before it ran into the Thames and to divert it east, by the force of gravity, to flow into the river beyond the edge of the city. The main sewers would be carried beneath two new embankments along the banks of the Thames, the Victoria Embankment on the north side of the river, and the Albert Embankment on the south side.

Six years in construction, the Bazelgette sewer system not only consigned "the Great Stink" to history, it also largely eliminated cholera in the city by separating sewage from the supply of drinking water.

FACT FILE
The Great Stink

Date: 1858

Location: London, England

Monarch: Queen Victoria

Issues: Overflowing sewers; the Thames was filthy; cholera, dysentery, and typhoid were rife in the city

Causes: New sanitary devices worsened the situation; London was overcrowded; birth rate increased; no sufficient investment in hygiene or infrastructure

Solutions: Heavy rains flushed out drains and rivers; in 1859, Joseph Bazalgette devised a system of underground and street sewers, separating sewage from drinking water, ridding the city of cholera

Great Chicago Fire

IN ANCIENT AND EARLY MODERN HISTORY, IT WAS NOT UNCOMMON FOR DISASTROUS FIRES TO SWEEP THROUGH CITIES. THESE WERE OFTEN MADE EVEN WORSE BY A COMBINATION OF WOODEN BUILDINGS AND RUDIMENTARY FIREFIGHTING SERVICES. HOWEVER, BY THE LATE NINETEENTH CENTURY, SUCH EVENTS WERE RELATIVELY RARE, YET IN 1871 A FIRE VIRTUALLY DESTROYED THE CITY OF CHICAGO.

Chicago, Illinois, situated on Lake Michigan, had since the 1830s grown to become a major trade link between the Great Lakes and the Mississippi River system. The opening up of the Midwest had increased its importance; the railroads from the West brought livestock—mainly cattle—from the western trailheads to Chicago's stockyards and slaughterhouses, making the city an essential link in a chain to supply food to the great cities of the East. By 1871, Chicago was a large, thriving, modern city, but it still had an air of the frontier town about it—as is reflected in the popular but inaccurate story that circulated for years that the great fire had been caused by a Mrs O'Leary's cow kicking over a lantern in a barn.

When the smoke cleared, the devastation was obvious...with 17,000 buildings burnt to the ground, and more than 100,000 people left homeless.

PERFECT FIRE WEATHER
The summer of 1871 had been exceptionally hot and dry in Chicago; from early July to the beginning of October less than 3 in (7.5 cm) of rain had fallen. In September 1871, just a month before the fire, the *Chicago Tribune* newspaper described the potential hazard of a city made up of so many "fire traps." Much of Chicago was made of wooden buildings that were now tinder-dry. Timber was so plentiful and cheap that the city's construction regulations and fire codes were rarely observed or implemented. Even many wealthy Chicagoans lived in wooden houses, while the large number of poor immigrants were packed into overcrowded wooden tenements. On the evening of October 7, 1871, firefighters successfully

extinguished a huge blaze in the city. They had barely returned to their fire stations the following evening, however—where they congratulated themselves on having averted a huge disaster—when another fire broke out. At about 9:00 p.m. on the night of October 8, 1871, another fire started, this time in a barn belonging to Irish immigrants Catherine and Patrick O'Leary.

A SLOW RESPONSE

The alarm was raised, but more than 40 minutes elapsed before any fire company received notice of the blaze. Even then, the fire companies, perhaps still exhausted from the previous day's work, were slow to respond. Somehow the fire

trucks were sent to the wrong address. The delay in reaching the barn allowed the fire to take hold. Fanned by strong south-westerly winds, the flames quickly spread to neighboring barns and sheds. Houses were soon alight, as was a church on the west side of the Chicago River. But the previous night's successful fire extinguishing operation meant that few people were unduly concerned about this new blaze.

Now flames spread across the Chicago river, leaping from ship to ship and across wooden bridges. The fire grew more

Chicago's strategic position as the focus of the railroad networks helped make it an important city in the United States at the time of the fire. However, wooden buildings and inadequate fire services were the city's downfall.

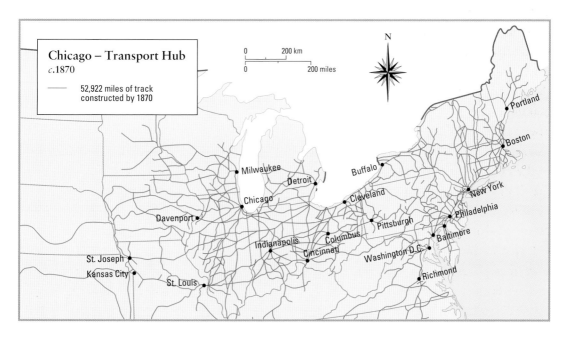

The Water Tower in Chicago is the second oldest water tower in the United States and was among the few buildings to survive the conflagration. This famous landmark is a symbol of old Chicago and the city's recovery from the fire.

the fire soon became too big to contain, especially after flames engulfed the city's waterworks on the north side of the river, leaving firefighters with no available water. Panic set in and people started to flee. Estimates suggest that up to one-quarter of the city's 330,000 residents left with whatever they could carry with them.

A WALL OF FIRE

Reports described a wall of fire 100 ft (30 m) tall racing through the downtown. The business district, with its offices, hotels, and city government buildings, was destroyed. Department stores, the city's opera house, churches, and theaters were all burnt to the ground. Chicago's affluent north side was also affected, as its mansions went up in smoke. The mayor, in an effort to stop the panic, put the city under martial law, under the direction of the distinguished Civil War Union general Philip Sheridan. Because no major disturbance materialized, martial law was lifted after just a few days.

intense and the flames climbed higher, setting rooftops ablaze far ahead of the main conflagration. The mayor of Chicago asked for help from neighboring cities, but

By Monday morning, a large part of the city had been razed to the ground; only stone and brick structures still stood. The fire continued to burn until a light rain started to fall on Monday evening. By early Tuesday morning, the blaze was finally extinguished, although burning embers meant that the extent of the damage could not be assessed for several days. When the smoke cleared, the devastation was clear. An area 4 miles (6.4 km) long and almost 1 mile (1.6 km) wide had been destroyed, with 17,000 buildings burnt to the ground and 100,000 people left homeless. Although only 120 bodies were found, it is believed that the true death toll was closer to 300. The cost of the damage was estimated to be $190 million.

NO CLEAR CAUSE

The cause of the fire has never been completely proven and there are many different theories. One thing is clear—Mrs O'Leary's cow was innocent. A reporter from the Chicago Republican newspaper admitted making up the story. The real culprit was almost certainly the combination of the long, hot summer and the wooden structures.

After the fire, newspaper photographers and reporters flocked to the city. Images of the fire's destructive path caused a great outpouring of sympathy. President Ulysses S. Grant sent a personal cheque for $1,000. The city was quickly rebuilt using much better construction methods and stricter fire codes. Today, the Chicago Water Tower is a rare survivor from the time before Great Chicago Fire and remains a symbol of the old city and its recovery from the disaster wreaked by the fire of 1871.

FACT FILE
Great Chicago Fire

Date: October 8, 1871

Point of Origin: Supposedly, a barn belonging to Catherine and Patrick O'Leary

Cause: The cause of the fire has never been established, but the contributing factors played a key role

Contributing Factors: Hot, dry summer; strong winds; wooden buildings; construction and fire regulations ignored; 40 minutes elapsed before fire services were alerted; they were slow to respond; fire trucks sent to the wrong address

Statistics: About 330,000 residents fled; 17,000 buildings burnt down; 100,000 people homeless; about 300 dead; $190 million in repairs

Recovery: The city was quickly rebuilt using stricter construction methods and fire codes

Battle of Little Bighorn

AS AMERICA CELEBRATED ITS CENTENARY, ITS CITIZENS WERE SHOCKED BY THE MASSACRE OF AN ELITE CAVALRY UNIT COMMANDED BY A UNION CIVIL WAR HERO, LT. COLONEL GEORGE A. CUSTER.

The origins of the Battle of the Little Bighorn date back to 1868. At Fort Laramie, Wyoming, the U.S. government had signed a treaty with the Great Plains peoples, including the Lakota, Sioux, and the Cheyenne, to allow a vast area of what is now South Dakota to be designated a Great Sioux reservation. For a time, Native Americans and white settlers coexisted in reasonable harmony. But the discovery of gold in the Black Hills in 1874 at the center of the proposed reservation changed all that. As the word rapidly spread, gold hunters rushed to the Black Hills, invading the Indian territory in direct contravention of the 1868 treaty.

GOLD FEVER AND RETALIATION

The U.S. Army tried but failed to stop the gold hunters, so the government attempted to buy the land from the Native Americans. This, too, proved unsuccessful. The Lakota and Cheyenne left the reserve and started carrying out retaliatory raids on settlers and travelers. In December 1875, the government ordered them to return to the reserve by January 31, 1876, or be treated as "hostile" people. When the date passed and they had not returned, the army was sent to enforce the order.

The army planned an advance in three columns. Brigadier General Alfred Terry ordered Lt. Colonel George Custer and the 7th Cavalry Regiment to proceed south along the Rosebud river while the other columns moved west toward the Bighorn and Little Bighorn rivers. The aim was to converge from all directions on the Native Americans who were expected to be encamped there.

TACTICAL MISTAKES

Custer sent out scouts who reported seeing a massive pony herd and a large Lakota, Cheyenne. and Arapaho encampment

The map shows the frontier Midwest and the territories held by Native American nations in the 1870s.

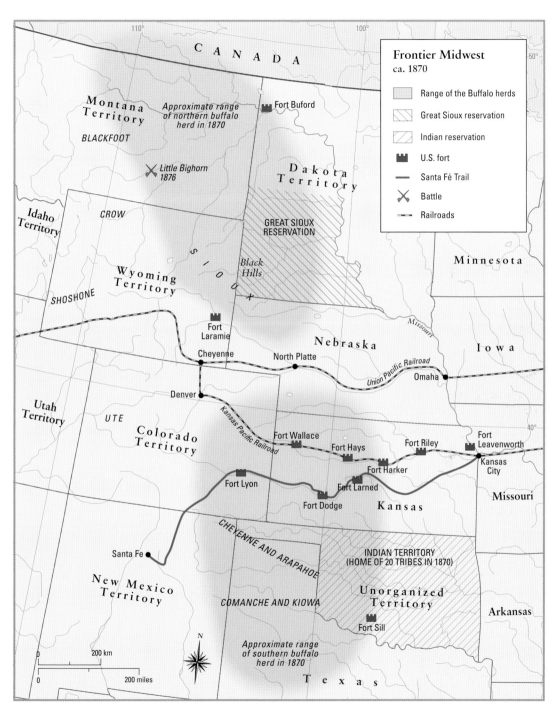

Frontier Midwest
ca. 1870

Range of the Buffalo herds
Great Sioux reservation
Indian reservation
U.S. fort
Santa Fé Trail
Battle
Railroads

CANADA

Montana Territory
Approximate range of northern buffalo herd in 1870

Fort Buford

BLACKFOOT

Little Bighorn 1876

Dakota Territory

Idaho Territory

CROW

S I O U X

GREAT SIOUX RESERVATION

Black Hills

Minnesota

Wyoming Territory

SHOSHONE

Fort Laramie

Cheyenne

North Platte

Nebraska

Union Pacific Railroad

Omaha

Iowa

Missouri

Denver

Kansas Pacific Railroad

Utah Territory

UTE

Colorado Territory

Fort Wallace

Fort Hays

Fort Riley

Fort Leavenworth

Kansas City

Fort Harker

Fort Lyon

Fort Larned

Fort Dodge

Kansas

Missouri

CHEYENNE AND ARAPAHOE

Santa Fe

New Mexico Territory

COMANCHE AND KIOWA

INDIAN TERRITORY (HOME OF 20 TRIBES IN 1870)

Unorganized Territory

Arkansas

Fort Sill

Approximate range of southern buffalo herd in 1870

200 km

200 miles

N

T e x a s

Little Bighorn battlefield near Crow Agency, Montana, is now a national monument serving as a memorial to those on both sides who fought and fell in the battle. Custer National Cemetery, on the battlefield, is part of the national monument.

some 15 miles (24 km) away. When Custer encountered a group of around 40 warriors close by, he mistakenly assumed they were on their way to warn the encampment. He issued an order to attack the camp immediately, although it had not been properly scouted. Working on wildly inaccurate estimates of the size of the force they faced, the army thought there were about 800 enemy combatants when the true number was closer to 2,000.

Custer divided his regiment into three, then compounded this major tactical error by being more concerned with preventing the Native Americans fleeing than working out how to fight them. He sent a unit under Captain Frederick Benteen to stop any escape through the upper valley of the Little Bighorn River. A second group, under Major Marcus Reno, was despatched to pursue the Indians, cross the river, and then attack the camp. He planned to lead his men in a simultaneous attack on the camp but failed to account for the terrain his men would have to cross, which was made up of bluffs and ravines.

On June 25, 1876, Reno and his 175 men attacked from the south, but they were forced to retreat after no more than ten minutes of fighting. The native warriors then turned their attention to Custer and his nearly 270 men, who had entered the camp from the north. They pushed Custer's men back on to a high ridge to the north. Another group of Lakota Sioux, led by the renowned warrior Crazy Horse, moved downstream and doubled back to ensnare Custer. The Native Americans fired at the soldiers with bows and arrows, but they were also armed with rapid-firing repeating rifles. Custer's single-shot Springfield carbines were no match for the superor weaponry. Custer had apparently been offered the Gatling gun, an early type of machine gun, but had rejected it.

THE "LAST STAND"

In less than an hour, according to some accounts, Custer and all his men lay dead. Reno and Benteen's men had joined forces and managed to fight off the native warriors until evening, and again in fierce fighting the next day. Whether Custer and his men made a "last stand" against the surrounding enemies is not known, as they all died. But the idea of a brave but doomed resistance to the mounted warriors became a part of Western legend. After the battle, the Indians moved through the battlefield, stripping the corpses and mutilating them, as was their custom. According to some reports, Custer's body was left unmutilated and unscalped, which some commentators claim was a mark of respect for his great fighting prowess.

The Battle of Little Bighorn caused consternation among white Americans celebrating the centennial and brought calls for vengeance for the death of a popular Civil War hero. Those who questioned Custer's actions were generally silenced by a campaign to preserve his reputation, although today it is widely accepted that he acted hastily and with little respect for the fighting skills of his enemy. For the Native Americans, the victory was a temporary triumph in their long struggle with the U.S. government, which bowed to popular anger and redrew the boundaries of the Sioux reserve, allowing white settlers into the Black Hills. The Native Americans at Little Bighorn packed up and left the area within 48 hours of the battle. After a further decade and a half of fighting with the U.S. Army, native resistance was finally overcome at Wounded Knee in 1890.

Commercial Disaster

WHEN THE TELEPHONE WAS INVENTED IN 1876, ITS PROMOTERS SAW AT ONCE THAT IT HAD THE POTENTIAL TO CHANGE THE WAY IN WHICH PEOPLE COMMUNICATED. THEY OFFERED TO SELL THE RIGHTS FOR THE NEW INVENTION TO THE THEN MASTERS OF THE COMMUNICATIONS BUSINESS, WESTERN UNION. IN ONE OF THE WORST COMMERCIAL MISTAKES IN BUSINESS HISTORY, WESTERN UNION DECLINED.

The invention of the telephone was mired in controversy and legal battles, but there is no dispute that the first person to be granted a patent for the invention was the Scottish-born inventor Alexander Graham Bell (1847–1922). In 1876, when Bell filed his patent application, the telegraph was by far and away the most successful method of long-distance communication in the United States, and the Western Union Telegraph Company the most successful firm in the sector.

Western Union had built its first telegraph lines in the 1850s. By 1860, they stretched from the east coast of the United States to the Mississippi River, and from the Great Lakes to the Ohio. The first transcontinental telegraph opened in 1861. By the mid-1870s, the Western Union Telegraph Company was worth $41 million—a vast sum at that time—up from just $385,700 only 18 years earlier. But communication by telegraph had its limitations. It could be used only for sending electrical transmissions in the form of Morse code messages, not for relaying actual speech.

Bell and his partners offered to sell the patent outright to Western Union for $100,000. Its president declined, arguing that the telephone was a gimmick.

COMMUNICATION FOR THE DEAF

Bell's interest in this area came from personal experience. His family had a long tradition of teaching elocution to deaf–mute people—his mother and future wife were both deaf—and he had studied acoustics. He felt that the electrical transmission of the voice would be a tremendous aid to deaf people, and was convinced there must be a way to do it. However, he could not work how this could be done until a chance meeting with Thomas A. Watson, an experienced electrical designer and mechanic, who provided the expertise Bell needed to convert his ideas into reality.

Bell was not the only inventor working on the telephone at that time. Indeed, he barely got there first. The unfortunate Elisha Gray actually arrived at the U.S. Patent Office on the same day as Bell, February 14, 1876, to file a patent caveat (a kind of holding application) for his invention, which was an acoustic telegraph that used a water transmitter. Although Bell applied a few hours later, his more formal patent was granted on March 7. This coincidence has ever since been the cause of much speculation and many conspiracy theories.

FIRST TELEPHONE CONVERSATION

Whatever the merits of Gray's invention, the spoils went to Bell who, on March 10, 1876, three days after receiving his patent, got his new invention to work for the first time. Speaking to his assistant in a neighboring office, he uttered the first words ever spoken on a telephone: "Mr Watson—Come here—I want to see you."

Bell next proved that the telephone could work over a long distance, and began showing his invention off to the wider scientific community. However, it was not until he exhibited his device at the U.S. Centennial Exposition in Philadelphia in 1876 that the telephone really took off. It initially received little attention until the Brazilian emperor Dom Pedro II visited the stand. His enthusiastic response helped Bell win the Gold Medal. Another royal who showed an interest in the invention was Queen Victoria of Great Britain. She demanded a private demonstration at Osborne House, her residence on the Isle of Wight and reportedly called the invention "extraordinary."

BELL TELEPHONE COMPANY

In 1877, the Bell Telephone Company was created to produce the new invention. The following year, Bell and his partners offered to sell the patent outright to Western Union for $100,000. Its president declined, arguing that the telephone was merely a gimmick and was not a viable nor an economic investment.

He soon realized his mistake. Only two years later, he was reported to have said that if he could acquire the patent for $25 million, he would consider it a bargain. Although Western Union bought other telephone patents filed by Elisha Gray, Thomas Edison, and Amos Dolbear, the U.S. Supreme Court awarded the basic patent right for the telephone to Alexander Graham Bell. Western Union was forced to sell its telephone patents to Bell and promise not to become involved in the telephone business.

For his part, Bell and his company had to agree to stay out of the telegraph business. That was all right by him because the telegraph market was about to lose a lot of its appeal. In fact, Bell came close to absorbing Western Union as a company—it was only prevented from doing so by the U.S. government's antimonopoly laws.

During the 1870s and 1880s, the Bell Telephone Company fought more than 580 cases relating to its patent and its right to produce the telephone. Its legitimacy was confirmed over and over again. The company only ever lost

Portrait of Alexander Graham Bell, inventor of the telephone.

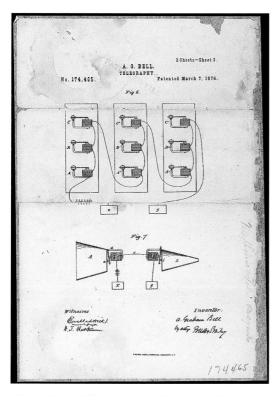

Alexander Graham Bell's patent application drawing for his telephone.

FACT FILE
Commercial Disaster

Invention: Telephone

Inventor: Alexander Graham Bell (1847–1922)

Disastrous Decision: When Bell offered to sell the patent outright to Western Union, the president declined

Consequences: Bell was awarded the patent right to the telephone; Western Union was forced to sell its telephone patents to Bell and agree not to become involved in the telephone business

Aftermath: Bell's company became America's largest corporation. Telephony was clearly the way of the 20th century

two minor cases. It wasn't until Alexander Graham Bell's second patent expired on January 30, 1894, that independent companies could finally compete with the Bell Telephone Company. Nonetheless, his company—which in 1885 was renamed the American Telephone and Telegraph Company—had by the early twentieth century become the largest corporation in the United States. The future was clear: telephony was the way of the twentieth century. Within the next century, the telephone would be an essential item in almost every household throughout the Western world. Bell would be astounded to see just how far the telephone has continued to develop in the 21st century, especially with the saturation that has been achieved by the cell phone across the globe.

Ghost Dance

BY THE 1880S, NATIVE AMERICANS FOUND THEIR TRADITIONAL LANDS AND LIFESTYLES UNDER INCREASING PRESSURE, AS WHITE SETTLEMENT SPREAD AND THE LAST REMAINING AREAS OF NORTH AMERICA BECAME PART OF THE UNITED STATES.

Native resistance resulted in violence against settlers and retaliation from the U.S. Army. Peace deals between the two sides inevitably favored the settlers. In desperation, the native peoples of the plains turned to a new religion to help resist the white man: the Ghost Dance. In its origins, the Ghost Dance was a ritual ceremony of the kind common to many Native American peoples, for whom it symbolized the sun's journey across the sky. But this version of the dance, and the beliefs that went with it, were new.

The dance was introduced by a self-appointed prophet, Jack Wilson of the Northern Paiute. Known by his native name of Wovoka, the prophet claimed to have had a vision on January 1, 1889, in which God showed him a beautiful land full of animals and told him that he must tell his people to live in harmony and peace with the white people. Furthermore, God told him that war was wrong and that his people must work and not lie or steal. If they lived according to these principles, all would be well and the living would be reunited with their dead ancestors.

Introduced by self-appointed prophet Jack Wilson ... he claimed to have had a vision in which God showed him a beautiful land full of animals ...

The Ghost Dance was the symbol of this new form of behavior. Wilson spread the word among the plains peoples, claiming to have the power to control the weather. If they all joined the Ghost Dance, then his vision would come to pass, and Wilson would be able to control the western United States while U.S. President Harrison remained God's deputy in the east.

THE DANCE SPREADS AND CHANGES
The Nevada Paiute first performed what they called the "Dance in a Circle" in

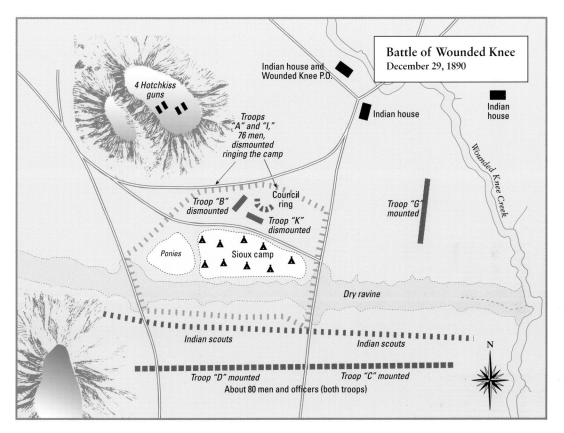

Battle of Wounded Knee
December 29, 1890

4 Hotchkiss guns

Indian house and Wounded Knee P.O.

Indian house

Indian house

Troops "A" and "I," 76 men, dismounted ringing the camp

Troop "B" dismounted

Council ring

Troop "K" dismounted

Troop "G" mounted

Wounded Knee Creek

Ponies

Sioux camp

Dry ravine

Indian scouts

Indian scouts

N

Troop "D" mounted

Troop "C" mounted

About 80 men and officers (both troops)

The Massacre at Wounded Knee was a shameful chapter in the story of U.S. government relations with Native Americans. There was some evidence to suggest that many of the soldiers who died were shot by friendly fire from their own side, the same cross fire that killed many women and children.

1889, and it swept through much of the western United States. It generally took the form of a group dancing in a circle with an individual in the middle, but also involved trances, exhortations, and prophesies. Tribes adapted the dance to their own belief systems, and it changed as it traveled, soon becoming an established part of many communities' rituals. It was among the Lakota Sioux, which had been displaced to the western plains from the Great Lakes region, that the Ghost Dance first moved away from Wilson's vision of nonviolence.

Kicking Bear, chief of the Lakota Sioux, preached that the Ghost Dance would not result in harmony with the white man; it would lead to the destruction of the white man. A flood would drown the settlers, while the Native Americans

An engraving of a Sioux warrior from the 1860s. Within 30 years of this engraving, the great Sioux Nation would be confined to reservations, its culture and its way of life destroyed.

spiritual powers, which would protect its wearers from bullets. Matters came to a head following the U.S. government's decision to break up the Lakota reserve in South Dakota and to give the land to homesteaders. Supported by the Bureau of Indian Affairs (BIA), the plan was to move the Lakota onto farms, where their children would be educated in white schools and they would practise Christianity; their own customs and practices would be outlawed.

By the end of the 1890 growing season, it was clear that inadequate rains and a hot summer had left the Lakota with insufficient crops to feed themselves; they faced a winter of starvation. To many in the U.S. government, this was confirmation of the widely held belief that Native Americans were lazy and work-shy. The Lakota turned to the Ghost Dance as a way out of their dire situation. Agents of the BIA saw the dance as hostile toward white people and

floated safely above, before returning to reclaim their rightful land. The Lakota also seized on another part of Wilson's prophecy. He had promoted the wearing of special Ghost Shirts, possibly influenced by the undergarments worn by elders of the Mormon Church. Among the Lakota, a belief grew that the Ghost Shirt had called for U.S. Army troops to be brought in to prevent it from being performed.

BATTLE OF WOUNDED KNEE

What followed was a controversial and shameful episode in U.S. history. Sitting Bull, the spiritual leader of the Hunkpapa Sioux, was arrested for failing to stop the Ghost Dance. In the melee that followed, Sitting Bull, a great warrior of Little Big Horn (and subsequently a performer in Buffalo Bill's Wild West Show) was shot dead by a U.S. lieutenant after one of his followers opened fire on the soldier.

Meanwhile, Big Foot, another important Sioux leader, was intercepted by U.S. troops on his way to meet with other Sioux chiefs. His band set up camp on the banks of Wounded Knee Creek in South Dakota on the evening of December 28, 1890. The next day, a Sioux warrior refused to give up his weapons to the troops. In the struggle that followed, a Sioux weapon was discharged, whereupon the U.S. soldiers opened fire. After a brief firefight, 25 U.S. soldiers and 153 Sioux lay dead. Most of the Native American casualties were women and children.

The clash at Wounded Knee was a disaster for both sides. In the outcry that followed, the U.S. government was forced to provide the Sioux with increased rations and to improve the financial compensation for their confiscated lands. For the peoples of the plains, the massacre was final proof that their faith in the Ghost Dance movement had been mistaken. Wounded Knee was the last armed clash of the campaign to force Native Americans onto reservations—the struggle was over and, far from Jack Wilson's utopian vision, native peoples faced a life confined to reservations on marginal land, where maintaining their traditional customs was almost impossible.

FACT FILE
Ghost Dance

Issue: Conflict between U.S. government and the Native Americans who wanted to be left in peace in the West

Final Conflicts: Spread of Ghost Dance movement among Native Americans

Disastrous Decision: Shooting of Sitting Bull, 1890; massacre of women and children at Wounded Knee, 1890

Consequences: Native Americans confined to increasingly smaller reserves

Aftermath: Native Americans for generations after lost their culture and their traditional ways of life, with tragic results

Twentieth Century

For sheer disaster on a global scale, the twentieth century stands out as particularly unfortunate. Two global wars, with unprecedented levels of death and destruction, marred the first half of the century. From Gallipoli to Dieppe, man's inhumanity to man was clearly demonstrated. But natural disasters and human error played their parts in making this a difficult period in which to live. The San Francisco earthquake and the sinking of the Titanic, the Triangle Shirtwaist fire and Prohibition, along with the Wall Street Crash, all provide examples of major disasters and mistakes.

San Francisco Earthquake

SAN FRANCISCO IS USED TO EARTHQUAKES. IT STANDS ON THE SAN ANDREAS FAULT, WHERE THE EARTH'S PLATES PUSH AGAINST ONE ANOTHER, REGULARLY SENDING SHOCKWAVES THROUGH THE GROUND. BUT THE EARTHQUAKE IN APRIL 1906 CAUSED MORE THAN 3,000 DEATHS AND DESTROYED SOME 25,000 HOUSES. IT ALSO CHANGED THE COURSE OF HISTORY FOR THE WESTERN UNITED STATES.

In 1906, San Francisco was little more than half a century old, but it had undergone huge growth following the California Gold Rush of 1849 and the completion of the first transcontinental railroad 20 years later. Its superb natural harbor and position facing the Pacific Ocean at the foot of the Coastal Mountains made it a transportation hub for the whole West Coast, and by the early 20th century, it was the largest and most prosperous city, not just in California but in the whole western United States, with a population of 410,000.

One sign of San Francisco's eminence as a cultural center was the presence in the city in 1906 of Enrico Caruso, the world-famous Italian tenor. He was visiting with the New York Metropolitan Opera to perform at San Francisco's Grand Opera House. Caruso had been so nervous about his trip to the "Wild West" that he had bought himself a gun and 50 rounds of ammunition for protection – but when he learnt that Mount Vesuvius had erupted near his hometown of Naples, in Italy, he concluded that San Francisco was a safer place to be. His performance of Don José in *Carmen* on April 17 had been greeted with great acclaim. But he was jolted awake the next morning in his suite in one of the world's biggest and most luxurious hotels, the Palace Hotel. This time the seismic

> *Thousands of terrified residents rushed into the streets, most still in their nightclothes. Some were struck by falling masonry from nearby buildings.*

The sheer destructive power of the San Francisco earthquake is clearly visible in this historic photograph taken in the aftermath of the quake. Many hundreds of buildings of brick, stone, and wood crumbled and fell, injuring and killing many of their inhabitants.

activity causing the rude awakening was an earthquake, not a volcano as he might have experienced in his home town.

THE CITY WAKES TO THE QUAKE

Shortly after 5:00 a.m., carthorses in the city market began to get restless and agitated and pull on their reins, while stray dogs started running through the streets. Then at 5:12 a.m., the earthquake struck. Thousands of terrified residents rushed into the streets, most still in their nightclothes. Some were struck and badly injured by falling masonry from the roofs and facades of nearby buildings. Others were killed in their beds as walls and ceilings collapsed. Countless small fires broke out as candles, gas lamps, and stoves toppled over, gas pipes ruptured, and power lines snapped in showers of sparks.

The earthquake measured 7.9 on the Richter scale (some reports suggest it might have been as high as 8.25). Although the epicenter lay some 2 miles (3.4 km) to the west of the city, in the Pacific Ocean, the earthquake still caused a land rupture some

296 miles (477 km) long. The shock was felt as far away as central Nevada to the east, Oregon to the north, and Los Angeles to the south. An initial shock of some 20–25 seconds was followed by a main shock that lasted for 42 seconds.

FIRE BUT NO WATER

The earthquake on its own had caused considerable damage, but the real threat now was fire. Beyond the stone buildings of the downtown district, much of the city's building stock was made of wood. After months of unseasonably warm weather, everything was tinder-dry, and the flames rapidly took hold.

The first fire broke out in a Chinese laundry directly opposite a fire station, but there was no water to put it out. Because the water pipes that led from the reservoirs 20 miles (32 km) outside of the city had broken, firefighters could not use the fire hydrants. The city's underground reservoirs and water cisterns soon ran dry. The steep streets made it difficult to raise much water pressure in fire hoses.

To make matters worse, only the fire chief, Dennis Sullivan, knew the locations of all the emergency cisterns—and he had been one of the first casualties of the disaster when a chimney from a neighboring hotel crashed through the roof of his fire station. With no chief, no alarm system, and no communications, the firefighters had no way of coordinating their response. In downtown San Francisco, a number of fires merged to form one huge blaze that destroyed a huge section of the city's center. Much of the destruction was deliberately caused by firefighters trying to create firebreaks. It would be four days before the fires were brought under control.

A DEVASTATED CITY

The official death toll from the earthquake and the subsequent inferno was just 700, but historians agree that the true number was probably nearer 3,000. More than 80 percent of the city's buildings had been destroyed, and around half the population, some 225,000 people, were left homeless. Many crowded into ferry terminals to escape across the bay to Oakland. Among them was Caruso, who fled the city by boat and train, vowing never to return. The Palace Hotel where he had been staying was designed to be fireproof and had its own water supply. But, with the water pipes ruptured and its tanks running dry, it, too, had been among the casualties of the disaster.

At 7.9 on the Richter scale, the earthquake was a major event that would have caused widespread destruction virtually anywhere. However, various factors exacerbated the catastrophe. First, much of the city was built on land reclaimed from the bay and sat on an unstable mixture of mud and sand. Buildings with shallow foundations simply toppled as the earthquake struck. The lack of water for firefighting was also a major factor, as was the exhaustion of the firefighters—many had been up all night dealing with a large fire—and the failure of the city's fire-warning system, which failed to sound the alarm after the quake broke 556 of the 600 batteries.

A REGIONAL RIVAL TAKES OVER

The earthquake changed the city forever. Thousands of residents who fled never returned, while many refugees were forced to live in tents in the city's parks for months. But lessons were learnt; when rebuilding began, San Francisco led the way in earthquake-proof buildings. However, it would cease to lead in other ways. Indeed, the city's prestige was damaged in a way that never truly recovered—the first decades of the 20th century saw the rise of a neighbor along the coast to the south that would usurp San Francisco's position as California's major city: Los Angeles.

FACT FILE
San Francisco Earthquake

Date: April 18, 1906

Time: 5:12 a.m.

Epicentre: Pacific Ocean, 2 miles(3.4 km) to the west of the city

Richter Magnitude Scale: 7.9

Contributing Factors: Much of the city sat on mud and sand; lack of water made firefighting difficult; firefighters were exhausted after fighting a fire the previous evening; the city's fire-warning system failed

Statistics: 700 recorded deaths, but probably nearer to 3,000; 225,000 homeless; more than 80 percent of buildings destroyed

Aftermath: The earthquake changed the city forever. Earthquake-proof buildings were the order of the day, but its reputation was irreparably damaged

Triangle Shirtwaist Fire

AT AROUND 4:45 P.M. ON MARCH 25, 1911, HUNDREDS OF YOUNG GIRLS AND WOMEN WERE PUTTING ON THEIR COATS TO LEAVE THE FACTORY WHERE THEY WORKED IN LOWER MANHATTAN. TWENTY MINUTES LATER, MANY OF THEM WERE LYING DEAD ON THE SIDEWALK BELOW THE BUILDING. THE TRAGEDY MARKED A TURNING POINT IN ATTITUDES TO WORKER SAFETY IN THE UNITED STATES.

The lower floors of the building on the corner of Greene Street and Washington Place, New York City, had closed at midday. The women left on the eighth to tenth floors were doing overtime to supplement their week of five-and-a-half, nine-hour days. They worked for the so-called "Shirtwaist Kings," Isaac Harris and Max Blanck, making tailored waists for women's shirts. Most were young Italian and Jewish immigrants who had recently arrived in the United States.

In 1910, the average American worker earned less than $15 a week, but new immigrants tended to earn far less; the shirtwaist makers were paid a piecework rate, according to how many shirts they finished. Such sweatshops flourished in U.S. cities that lacked labor laws, trades unions, or health and safety rules. Inside the shirtwaist factory, the floor was covered in fabric scraps and the bins were filled with scraps of material, all of which were highly flammable. By the time someone shouted "fire!" as the girls got ready to leave for the day, smoke was billowing out of the windows on the eighth floor.

> The door to the staircase had been deliberately locked ... to stop workers stealing from the company. Nineteen bodies would be found melted against the locked door.

TRAPPED BY THE FLAMES

Panic set in immediately. There were 27 water buckets on the eighth floor,

The rapid spread of the fire and the pile of bodies on the sidewalks prevented firefighting engines from getting closer to the building.

but the fire spread too quickly for them to be of any use. The numerous exits became impassable, and intense heat soon prevented the women from reaching the Greene Street staircase and fire escape.

Even more shameful was the fact that the door to the Washington Place staircase had been deliberately kept locked by the owners in order to stop workers from stealing from the company. Nineteen bodies would be found melted against the locked door.

The girls who did reach the Greene Street staircase climbed onto the roof, where about 150 of them escaped by climbing up a ladder lowered by students from the adjacent New York University law building, which was 12 ft (3.6 m) higher. When flames made the Greene Street staircase impassable, girls climbed onto the one external fire escape. It was already weak; now a combination of heat from the fire and the weight of those trying to escape made it collapse. Around 20 girls plunged to their deaths, falling 100 ft (30 m) to the sidewalk below.

Other girls were luckier. The elevator operators Joseph Zitto and Gaspar Mortillalo risked their lives by taking the elevators up to the eighth and ninth floors to carry down as many as 15 girls on each trip, some with their clothes and hair smoldering from the fire. They continued until the heat of the fire caused the elevator rails to buckle. Desperate girls flung themselves into the shafts in a hopeless attempt to ride down on the elevator roof. Zitto described how blood ran down the sides of his elevator.

PLUNGING TO THEIR DEATHS

While horrified spectators watched, some 40 girls chose to jump from the windows to certain death instead of staying on the burning floors. Bodies piled up on the sidewalks below, preventing firefighters getting their horse-drawn engines close to the burning building. Engine Company 72 was only six streets away, but neither the firefighters' water stream nor their ladders reached beyond the seventh floor. Some girls tried to jump onto the extended ladders, but all missed and they too fell to their deaths.

The final death toll was 146: some 129 women and girls and 17 men, who also worked in the factory, mainly as garment cutters. These included three men who attempted to form a human chain between an eighth floor window and a window in the adjacent building. A few girls successfully crossed to the window before the men lost their balance and fell to their deaths.

Eventually, firefighters were able to get up the stairs and put out the fire, but it was some time before the building cooled sufficiently to allow the bodies inside to be retrieved. The steel-and-concrete structure withstood the blaze and still stands today. The cause of the fire has never been wholly explained; but a likely explanation is that someone was smoking illegally—smoking was officially banned in the factory—and threw the cigarette stub into a bin full of cloth, setting the contents alight.

MAKING THE CITY SAFER

Both of the "Shirtwaist Kings" were at the factory that day, with their children. They escaped the blaze—and they also escaped any blame for making the tragedy worse. On December 28, 1911, both were acquitted of wrongdoing, specifically of having locked the door to prevent theft, thereby blocking an escape route. In 1913, however, they lost a civil suit and were forced to pay 23 families a sum of $75 compensation per victim.

The public outcry at the deaths of so many young girls—in full view of the horrified crowds below—led the New York authorities to bring in new labor and health and safety laws. As a direct result of the tragedy, the New York Fire Department inspected the city's factories and found at least another 200 that risked a similar blaze. Fire sprinklers, alarm systems, and fireproofing were made compulsory in factories. Doors could no longer be kept locked while workers were inside, and access and exits were improved. More generally, legislation was passed preventing women and children from working such long hours. The deaths of so many immigrants, then at the margins of society, had forced the creation of some of the earliest and most significant workplace legislation in U.S. history.

FACT FILE
Triangle Shirtwaist Fire

Date: March 25, 1911

Time: 4:40 p.m.

Location: Asch Building (eighth, ninth, and tenth floors occupied by the Triangle Waist Company, a garment factory

Cause of fire: Speculation that a cigarette in combination with combustible materials

Contributing Factors: Exit doors were locked. Fire spread too rapidly

Statistics: 146 people killed, some from fire, others from falling or jumping from the building

Consequences: Revised labor, health and safety laws; stricter regulations for factories; American Society of Safety Engineers was founded in 1911 as a consequence

Sinking of the *Titanic*

EVEN A HUNDRED YEARS AFTER THE EVENT, THE SINKING OF THE "UNSINKABLE" *TITANIC* ON ITS MAIDEN VOYAGE EXERCISES A POWERFUL GRIP ON THE POPULAR IMAGINATION. SOME 1,500 PEOPLE LOST THEIR LIVES WHEN THE SHIP STRUCK AN ICEBERG ON APRIL 14, 1912, THE WORST PEACETIME MARITIME DISASTER.

At the beginning of the 20th century, the transatlantic liner business had never been busier or more competitive. Shipping companies built bigger and faster ships to attract passengers traveling to and from North America. The White Star Company, the owners of the *Titanic* and her sister ship, the *Olympic*, were determined to make their ships the last word in luxury.

THE WORLD'S MOST LUXURIOUS LINER

Thomas Andrews, the chief designer of the *Titanic*, built not just the biggest liner in the world, but also the most luxurious and comfortable. The ship boasted remarkable new technology, including a double hull divided into 16 (supposedly) watertight bulkhead compartments. Four of the compartments could fill with water and the ship would still float. The rival Cunard line might have faster ships, but the *Titanic* was by far the largest ship

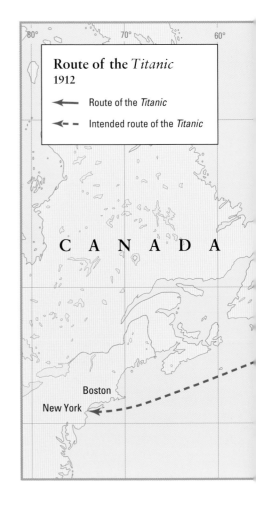

Route of the *Titanic*
1912

⟵ Route of the *Titanic*

◄- - Intended route of the *Titanic*

CANADA

Boston

New York

The ship had three classes of travel. The 329 first-class passengers enjoyed Turkish baths, a heated saltwater swimming pool, a gymnasium, a library, a billiards room, grand dining rooms, and spacious promenade decks. One way the decks had been made so big was by cutting down on the number of lifeboats on board; these were deemed to be unnecessary since the ship was supposed to be unsinkable. Travel conditions were much more basic for the 710 third-class passengers, most of whom were poor immigrants seeking a new life in the United States. The difference in

The fateful maiden voyage of the passenger liner, the Titanic, *has become the subject of many books, movies, and exhibitions.*

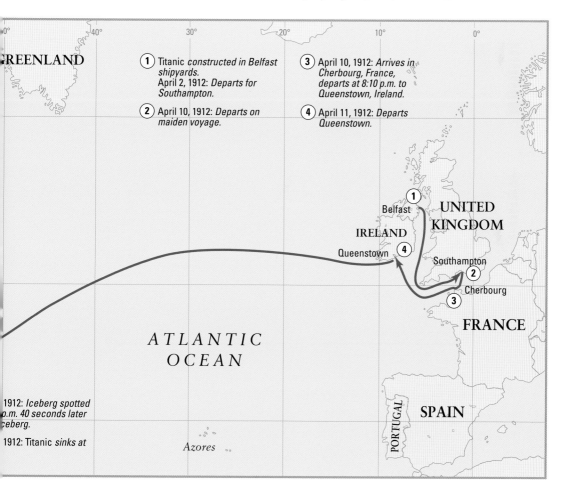

40°   40°   30°   20°   10°   0°

GREENLAND

① Titanic *constructed in Belfast shipyards.*
April 2, 1912: *Departs for Southampton.*

② April 10, 1912: *Departs on maiden voyage.*

③ April 10, 1912: *Arrives in Cherbourg, France, departs at 8:10 p.m. to Queenstown, Ireland.*

④ April 11, 1912: *Departs Queenstown.*

Belfast

UNITED KINGDOM

IRELAND

Queenstown   ④

Southampton   ②

Cherbourg

③

FRANCE

ATLANTIC OCEAN

PORTUGAL   SPAIN

1912: *Iceberg spotted* p.m. 40 seconds later *ceberg.*

1912: Titanic *sinks at*

Azores

facilities was reflected in the price of a ticket: a first-class ticket cost $4,350 (even by today's standards a lot of money, but in 1912 it was an enormous sum of money); a third-class ticket, on the other hand, was around $40.

CROSSING THE ATLANTIC

The *Titanic* sailed from Southampton on Wednesday, April 10, 1912 to collect passengers in France and Ireland. By April 12, it was steaming across the Atlantic at 21 knots, due to arrive in New York five days later. By the Sunday, the ship had increased its speed to 22.5 knots, but the temperature was falling. The crew received messages from other ships in the area warning of icebergs ahead, but the junior wireless operator, Jack Phillips, interrupted the warnings to carry on sending his backlog of messages on behalf of the first-class passengers.

If he ever got the warnings, Captain Edward Smith, on his last voyage before retiring from the White Star Line, ignored them. There is some argument that he was influenced by the White Star chairman J. Bruce Ismay, who was onboard, to sail as quickly as possible to make a good time and impress the passengers.

The convention for evacuation was women and children first. Most men stayed to face their doom, apart from crew members who took charge of the lifeboats ...

ICEBERG SIGHTED

Late that night, the lookouts in the crow's nest—they had no binoculars—spotted an iceberg looming out of the darkness. They sounded the warning bell at 11:40 p.m. The first officer swung the ship to the left to avoid a head-on collision but the iceberg grazed along the ship's right side, tearing a 300 ft (90 m) gash in its metal hull just beneath the waterline.

The impact seemed gentle; most passengers had no idea the ship had been hit. But when the designer Thomas Andrews toured the lower decks to assess the damage, he reported to Captain Smith that the ship would sink within a few hours. The tear in the *Titanic's* hull was so long that even its watertight compartments could not save it. As the bow of the ship was pulled deeper and deeper underwater, seawater would inevitably flow from one compartment to the next.

As the wireless room began broadcasting distress messages, the crew began to get passengers into the lifeboats. But the lifeboats onboard had space for just 1,178 people, while the ship was carrying 2,223 passengers and crew. To make things worse, there had been no lifeboat drills. Smith's officers did not know how best to load and release the boats. They wrongly believed, for example, that the lifeboats could not be lowered fully loaded. Many were launched half-empty; one had only 12 passengers when it was designed to hold 40 people

WOMEN AND CHILDREN FIRST

The convention for evacuation was "women and children first." Most of the men stayed to face their doom, apart from those crew members who took charge of the lifeboats and White Star chairman J. Bruce Ismay, who spent the rest of his life branded as a coward for taking a place in a lifeboat. There were many tales of touching partings between men and their families, and of women who chose to stay with their husbands. The ship's band continued to play on deck to keep up the spirits of the passengers left behind.

Third-class passengers died in proportionally greater numbers than other classes. All the children in first and second class survived, but only one-third of the children in third class made it to safety. Almost all the women in first class survived, while nearly half of those in third class did not. However, stories about those in steerage being locked in are unfounded. The figures probably simply reflect the fact that they would have had much farther to travel up through the ship to the deck and safety of the lifeboats.

HELP ARRIVES

Meanwhile, the closest ship to the *Titanic*, the *Californian*, had switched off its wireless for the night. Instead, the first vessel to answer the distress calls was the *Carpathia*, five hours' sailing away. By the time the *Carpathia* arrived, the *Titanic* had snapped in two, and the bow had pulled the ship almost vertical, and had sunk. Thomas Andrews was last seen below decks, staring at a large mural. Captain Smith also went down with his ship.

No one could survive for long in the freezing sea. The *Carpathia* picked up 705 survivors from the lifeboats and headed into New York, where it docked on April 18. Although news had filtered out, it was only then that the full extent of the disaster became clear.

The public inquiries that followed in New York and London identified key issues to be redressed—from now on ships had to carry enough lifeboats for every person onboard; lifeboat drills were made mandatory; and ships' hulls had to be built stronger. New shipping lanes were established in the North Atlantic under the control of the International Ice Patrol, whose job it was to track icebergs and warn shipping in good time.

Gallipoli

IN THE FIRST FALL OF WORLD WAR I, THE ALLIES CAME UP WITH A PLAN TO
ATTACK THE OTTOMAN EMPIRE. THE ALLIED LANDINGS ON THE GALLIPOLI
PENINSULA WERE A TRAGIC FAILURE THAT ENTERED THE NATIONAL MYTHS OF
AUSTRALIA AND NEW ZEALAND, AND HERALDED THE EMERGENCE OF THE
TURKISH NATIONAL HERO KEMAL ATATURK.

F rench war planners, eager to relieve
pressure on the Western Front,
were the first to suggest an attack
on the Ottoman Empire, but the most
enthusiastic supporter of the proposal
was Winston Churchill, First Lord of the
Admiralty. The target was the Dardanelles,
the 30 mile (50 km) sea passage dividing
Europe from Asia, which leads from the
Mediterranean to the Ottoman capital
Istanbul, and then
on to the Black Sea.
The entrance to the
Dardanelles was
guarded on the Asian
shore by the fort at
Kum Kale and on the
European side by various positions along
the narrow Gallipoli peninsula.

The British First Sea Lord, Admiral
Fisher, urged a joint military and naval
attack—which he believed had a good
chance of succeeding as long as it
happened quickly, but the Turks were
already strengthening their defenses. Even
though Allied discussions delayed the plan,
Churchill pushed ahead anyway, organizing
a fleet of old battleships, and gathering
troops for the assault, including the
Australian and New Zealand Army Corps
(ANZAC), which were in Egypt, waiting
to be moved to France.

*The plan depended entirely on
surprise. The Turks had been
digging trenches above the landing
beaches since the Allied failure to
force the Dardenelles ...*

THE PUSH BEGINS

The success of any
landing depended
on an initial naval
operation, but it
seemed to the Allies
that a coordinated push could force its
way through the Dardanelles past the
antiquated Turkish defenses. But when
that push began on March 18, it ended in
disaster, with three battleships sunk and

three more put out of action. The attempt to force the channel was abandoned; the mines remained unswept and the shore batteries were still in place.

The Allied commanders decided the landings should still go ahead. They moved their five divisions to the Greek island of Lemnos as stores and landing craft were hastily assembled for a landing on April 25. The destination was the Gallipoli Peninsula on the European shore. The ANZACs would land on the west coast, with British forces landing at five beaches around the tip of peninsula at Cape Helles, below the Turkish minefields.

The plan depended entirely on surprise. The Turks had been digging trenches above the landing beaches since the Allied failure to force the Dardanelles, and most beaches were now covered in barbed wire. The Allied force was not large enough to launch simultaneous attacks, which would have prevented the Turks from reinforcing and resupplying the peninsula. The only hope of success was that the Turks would be slow to react to any landings.

LANDINGS AT ANZAC COVE

On April 25, 200 merchant ships supported by a naval fleet headed for Cape Helles and what soon became known as ANZAC Cove. At 5:00 a.m. a bombardment began and the Allied

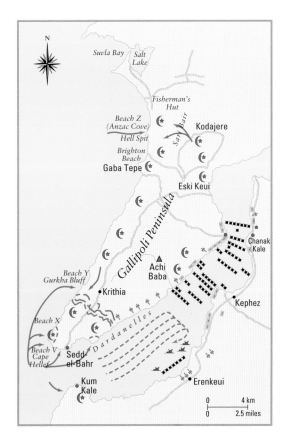

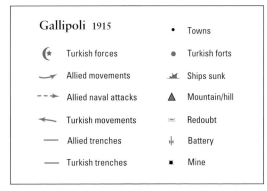

Gallipoli 1915			
☾	Turkish forces	•	Towns
⌒	Allied movements	●	Turkish forts
- - ►	Allied naval attacks	⚔	Ships sunk
◄	Turkish movements	▲	Mountain/hill
—	Allied trenches	▭	Redoubt
—	Turkish trenches	⊹	Battery
		✶	Mine

The Gallipoli campaign was a black spot on the career of rising star Winston Churchill and a bright beginning for Turkish officer Mustafa Kemal.

For Australians and New Zealanders, ANZAC and Gallipoli represent the sacrifice of their young men in what was to be a futile attempt to gain a foothold on the Dardanelles during the early stages of World War I. Anzac Day is celebrated in both countries on April 25.

rowboats set out for shore. At ANZAC Cove, the 12,000 ANZACs landed a mile north of their intended destination for reasons that are not fully understood. The new landing site was a small bowl beneath steep slopes that rose to high ridges overlooking the beach on three sides. It was vital to seize the high ground quickly, but after a virtually unopposed landing, it soon became clear why the defenses were so light. The men trying to climb up to the Sari Bair ridge became bogged down among the thick scrub and steep gullies. Some gullies led to dead ends, while others became blocked by huge bottlenecks of men. As Turkish defenders began to gather (led by an astute officer named Mustafa Kemal, who realized that his superiors were wrong to assume that the landings were a feint) the ANZACs were left clinging to the hillsides. At Cape Helles, 10 miles (16 km) to the south, some of the five landings were unopposed, while just over the headland other divisions fought for their lives against entrenched Turkish defenders. The most promising site was Y Beach, from where it would be possible to get behind the Turkish defenses. Although the landing was unopposed, the attackers failed to prepare for the inevitable counterattack. When it came that evening, it left the British clinging to the coast. The attack was abandoned later in the day.

Of the 30,000 men who landed on the first day, there had been 2,000 casualties among the ANZACs and another 2,000 at Helles. The Allies were digging entrenchments, but they were still on the beaches. Mustafa Kemal's quick thinking had prevented them from capturing the high ground—and in doing so had doomed the Gallipoli campaign to failure.

STALEMATE AND RETREAT

With both sides entrenched, and neither having the strength to defeat the other, the situation reached a stalemate that resembled the Western Front. The campaign became largely static, although there were many acts of gallantry among the Allied troops who made sporadic, doomed uphill attacks toward the Turkish positions. Disease and exposure made life hard for both sides. Eventually, the campaign was quietly abandoned. On December 19, the two Allied forces were withdrawn from under the noses of the Turkish defenders at ANZAC Cove, and from Cape Helles a few weeks later. The withdrawal was the best-managed part of the entire campaign.

The Allies had been in Gallipoli for some eight months, and had achieved precisely nothing. They had lost about 70,100 men—including 8,700 Australians and 2,700 New Zealanders—compared with Turkish losses of about 60,000.

Churchill's reputation suffered as a consequence of his unwavering support for the plan. Mustafa Kemal, on the other hand, began his inexorable rise that would result in him becoming the leader of post-war Turkey under the title Kemal Atatürk, "Father of the Turks." For Australians and New Zealanders an important part of their national myth was born, and is still celebrated every April 25 on ANZAC Day to mark the sacrifice of the youth of their respective nations.

Battle of the Somme

THE FIRST DAY OF THE BRITISH OFFENSIVE ON THE SOMME, JULY 1, 1916, HAS BECOME A SYMBOL OF THE FUTILITY OF WAR AND SHORTHAND FOR THE SACRIFICE OF GALLANT SOLDIERS BY INCOMPETENT GENERALS. SOME 20,000 MEN DIED IN ONE DAY FOR VIRTUALLY NO GAIN.

By the spring of 1916, the trenches stretching along the Western Front in Flanders and north-east France had been in place for nearly two years. Neither side was close to breaking the deadlock. Now the Allies planned to put pressure on the Central Powers by coordinating offensives on the Eastern Front and in northern Italy, hoping that a "big push" on the Western Front would relieve some of the pressure on the fortress town of Verdun, where the French army was fending off a concerted German attack. The push would come on the river Somme, where the French and British sectors of the front line met. Although conceived as a French operation, the Somme attack would now be led by the British.

THE "PALS" BATTALIONS

The British commander-in-chief Sir Douglas Haig thought an offensive would be more effective in Flanders to the north,

but his political masters in London told him to cooperate with the French. Haig set about preparing for an offensive in the high empty region, which had not been fought over since the first weeks of the war. He turned the area into an enormous military camp and prepared the infrastructure to support a huge advance: new roads, arms dumps, encampments, even a water supply, because there was not enough in the area to support an army. That army —20 divisions—was mainly new to the war. Most were 'Kitchener' volunteers who had joined up in answer to an appeal from Lord Kitchener (his face appeared on the poster bearing the motto: "Britain Needs You"). They were encouraged to form "Pals" or "Chums" battalions, serving with their friends or neighbours. But neither their infantry

The changing frontlines throughout the battle of the Somme in 1916, when hundreds of thousands of young men on both sides lost their lives.

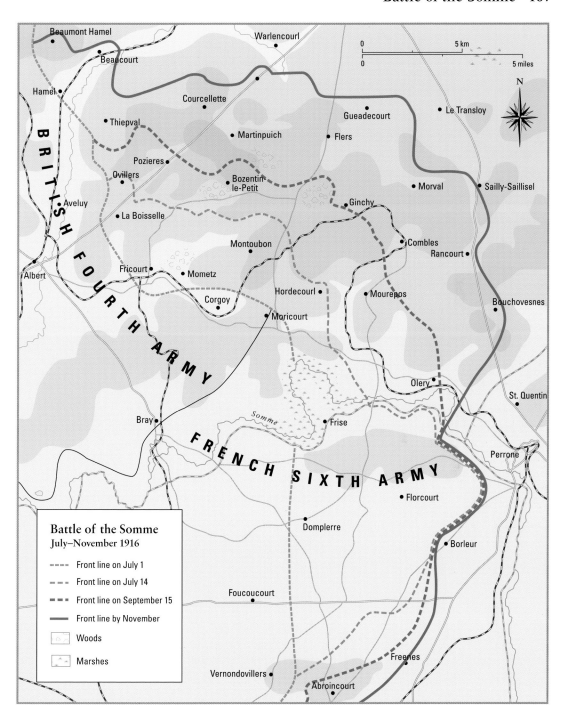

Beaumont Hamel

Warlencourl

0   5 km
0   5 miles

N

Beaucourt

Hamel

B R I T I S H

Courcellette

Thiepval

Gueadecourt

Le Transloy

Martinpuich

Flers

Pozieres

Ovillers

Bozentin-
le-Petit

Morval

Sailly-Saillisel

Aveluy

F O U R T H

La Boisselle

Ginchy

Montoubon

Combles

Rancourt

Albert

Fricourt

Mometz

A R M Y

Corgoy

Hordecourl

Mourepos

Bouchovesnes

Moricourt

Olery

St. Quentin

Bray

F R E N C H   S I X T H   A R M Y

Somme

Frise

Perrone

Florcourt

Domplerre

Borleur

Battle of the Somme
July–November 1916

- - - - -   Front line on July 1

- - - -   Front line on July 14

▬ ▬ ▬   Front line on September 15

▬▬▬▬   Front line by November

Woods

Marshes

Foucoucourt

Freenes

Vernondovillers

Abroincourt

One of the many trenches on the Western Front, which have been restored and serve as a reminder of the grimness of trench warfare.

and demoralize the troops. As the bombardment died away on July 1, some 19 British divisions north of the Somme and three French divisions to the south would go over the top. Given the men's inexperience, he wanted to prevent them from stopping to cover each other's advance with rifle fire so he ordered them to advance in carefully ordered lines. Many were assured that the weight of the artillery preparation would prevent the Germans from manning their defenses.

OVER THE TOP

At zero hour on July 1, 1916, whistles blew along the front and the officers and men of the BEF started to scramble forward. Some 17 British divisions left their trenches to go "over the top," each carrying the 60 lb (27 kg) of equipment they were thought to need for the task. Only 5 of the 17 reached the German positions; the rest never got out of no-man's land. They faced one of the strongest German positions on the whole Western Front, with dugouts nearly 30 ft (10 m) deep where the defenders had waited out the preliminary barrage with impunity. Far from cutting the barbed wire, the British shells merely threw it into even thicker tangles. When the barrage, which was supposed to clear the way for the infantry lifted too soon, the Germans simply manned the parapets of the trenches

nor their supporting artillery had any experience.

Haig planned a week-long artillery bombardment, a million shells that would cut the barbed wire in no-man's land, knock out German artillery,

and opened fire on the men still struggling to get through the wire. In places, they had actually stopped shooting when it was clear their positions were in
no danger.

A GENERATION CUT DOWN

The result was carnage. Many of the dead were killed by German machine guns on land the British already held before the attack began. Of the 100,000 men who went over the top, one-fifth—20,000 men—never returned. Another 40,000 were wounded. Some battalions ceased to exist. Haig, possibly not realizing the full extent of the losses, reported: "The enemy has undoubtedly been severely shaken and he has few reserves in hand." In fact, German losses were only about one-tenth of those of the British—6,000 men—and more reserves arrived during the day.

The offensive on the Somme had months to go. By the end of July, the Germans had lost 160,000 men; the French and British 200,000. The French had made some inroads, but the front had moved no more than 3 miles (5 km) in the month. In November, when the offensive officially ended, the farthest line of advance was 7 miles (11 km) ahead of where it had been on July 1. The Germans had lost 160,000 men, and the Allies well over that figure.

Some modern military experts believe that Haig could have done nothing different. Large numbers of casualties were inevitable when many thousands of men in cloth uniforms advanced into a hail of fire from machine guns and rifles. But in many ways that seems an inadequate excuse. The Kitchener system meant that the young men of entire villages or city districts were cut down together, leaving whole communities devastated. The popular perception came to be of a generation of youth cut down on one morning in July. Never did it seem more apt to describe the British army as "lions led by donkeys."

FACT FILE
Battle of the Somme

Date: July 1–November 18, 1916

Historical Context: World War I

States Involved: France, England, and Allies; Germany

Outcome: Decisive German victory

Statistics: French and British lost 20,000 men on July 1; Germans lost 6,000; by end of July, Germany had lost 160,000 while French and English 200,000

Consequences: The Kitchener system meant that young men from the same villages would be killed together, leaving whole communites bereft of young men

Prohibition

WHEN A BAN ON THE SALE OF ALCOHOL CAME INTO EFFECT AT MIDNIGHT ON JANUARY 17, 1920, MEMBERS OF THE TEMPERANCE MOVEMENT ACROSS THE UNITED STATES CELEBRATED VICTORY IN ITS CAMPAIGN TO SET THE COUNTRY ON A PATH OF VIRTUE. HOWEVER, IT WAS MORE OF A CASE OF BE CAREFUL WHAT YOU WISH FOR.

To the horror of most Americans, the following decade brought a huge increase in criminal activity, because the trade in alcohol went underground and gangsters took control of the liquor trade. There was also no significant reduction in the consumption of alcohol. The "noble experiment" had proved a complete failure. The United States' attitude toward alcohol had been complicated since Independence. While bars and saloons flourished, moral disapproval—mainly from Methodists, Lutherans, and other Protestants—coalesced into a number of temperance societies, the first of which appeared in 1808 in Saratoga, New York.

As the movement spread during the 19th century, people sided with either the "drys" or "wets," and states followed, introducing legislation to either allow or ban the sale of alcohol. Many women became "drys," believing that drunkenness destroyed families and a man's ability to work and seeing saloons as dens of inequity, full of prostitutes and criminals. For such women, temperance was often simply one factor in a wider program of reform, which also included such issues as the abolition of slavery and women's rights.

Among the notable temperance campaigners was Carrie Nation from Kansas. In 1880, her home state had passed a prohibition law, but few people paid it any attention and taverns still operated openly. Taking the law into her own hands in 1899, Nation took a hatchet and smashed up several local bars, making her front-page news and helping promote the movement.

RISE OF THE "DRYS"

By the beginning of the 20th century, the

The spread of Prohibition across the United States in the years between 1904 and 1915 made possible the legislation to impose temperance laws in many counties across the country.

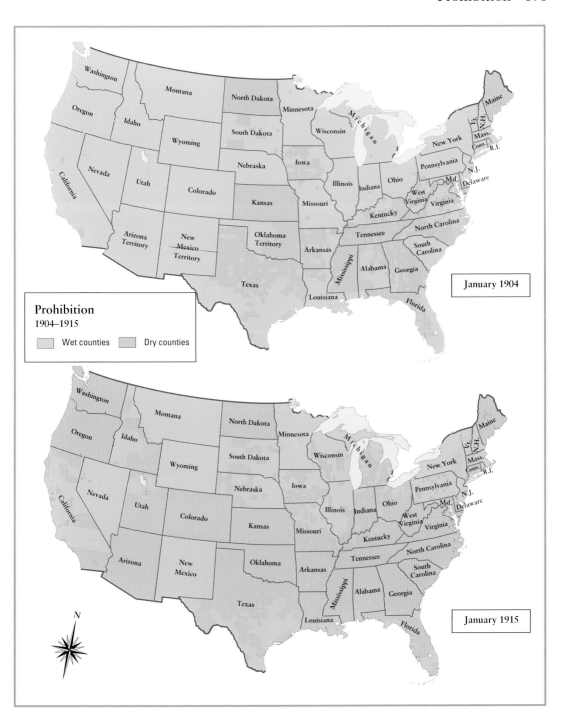

Prohibition
1904–1915

Wet counties   Dry counties

January 1904

January 1915

N

"drys" were gaining momentum on a state level, but had yet to make any national impact. Many people joined the "drys" out of disgust at the unsavory conditions in many taverns rather than out of a dislike of alcohol. The Anti-Saloon League, formed in 1895, and later supported by numerous millionaires, including Henry Ford, Andrew Carnegie, and John D. Rockefeller, bombarded the public with calls to ban alcohol. The brewery owners, concerned about their $2 billion yearly sales, fought back before a decisive event occurring thousands of miles away had a direct influence on their business. World War I (1914–1918) saw a huge rise in anti-German sentiment in the United States. Because many brewers in the country were of German origin, drinking beer became seen as unpatriotic.

Many of our best citizens have openly ignored Prohibition; respect for the law has been greatly lessened; and crime has increased to a level never seen before.

A move to introduce a new constitutional amendment to ban the production and sale of alcohol was passed by the Senate in August 1917, on condition that it would only become law if 36 of the 48 states ratified it within seven years. Few people imagined that would happen, but it did. The 18th Amendment forbade the manufacture, sale, transportation, import and export of intoxicating liquor in the United States. The law that brought it into effect—the Volstead Act, named for Congressman Andrew Volstead of Minnesota—was introduced on October 27, 1919.

The act had many loopholes. It did not ban drinking alcohol bought before the ban, for example, so by the time it came into force at midnight on January 17, 1920, people had stocked up. The manufacture of alcohol under 0.5 percent proof was still permitted, and alcohol could still be bought for medicinal, industrial, and religious purposes. Enforcing the law relied on 1,500 poorly paid federal agents.

BOOTLEG USA

Over the next decade, armed gangs took control of the alcohol business and made billions from illegal sales of alcohol smuggled in from Canada, Mexico. and the West Indies. To begin with, the gangsters were seen as meeting a legitimate need, and many lawmakers turned a blind eye. This was the brief period known as the "Roaring Twenties." Speakeasies and "blind pigs"— private clubs that were supposedly secret— sprang up in every major city and small town. Some were dives, but others were elegant and sophisticated establishments, such as New York's 21 Club, which attracted artists, writers, musicians, members of high society, and even the city mayor Jimmy Walker. Speakeasies were also a center of the growing jazz movement.

The crime wave around this illegal trade soon spiraled. In cities such as Chicago and Detroit, mobsters paid off the police and took control. In Cleveland, Ohio, so many gangsters were shot at one particular road junction it became known as "Bloody Corner." Each major city had its supreme mobster: in New York it was Frank Costello; in Philadelphia, Maxie Hoff; and in Kansas City, Chester LeMare.

The most infamous gangster of all was "Scarface" Al Capone of Chicago. Capone was responsible for the infamous St. Valentine's Day Massacre of 1929, when members of his gang, some disguised as policemen, machine-gunned to death members of the rival gang of Bugs Moran. The shootout shocked the country. As the decade wore on, it was apparent that the government was losing out to organized crime. Capone alone was said to earn $100 million a year from selling illegal liquor.

END OF THE EXPERIMENT
Three weeks after the St. Valentine's Day Massacre, Herbert Hoover was elected the thirty-first president. That same year, the

United States plunged into an economic depression and people became more concerned with feeding their families than with supporting temperance. In 1931, 90,000 bootleggers were arrested, yet this barely made a dent on the industry. Common sense said that the 18th Amendment had to go—the only time an amendment has been repealed.

Franklin D. Roosevelt, a reformist Democrat, came to the White House in 1933 with a mandate to repeal the act: he told his aides, "I think this would be a good time for beer." Between April 10, 1933 when Michigan became the first state to repeal the 18th Amendment by ratifying the 21st Amendment, and December 5 when Utah became the last, most states made alcohol legal again (a few—Kentucky, Kansas, Oklahoma, and Mississippi—chose to remain dry). Prohibition was at an end. The prominent "dry" John D. Rockefeller bemoaned its effects: "Drinking has generally increased; the speakeasy has replaced the saloon; a vast army of lawbreakers has appeared; many of our best citizens have openly ignored Prohibition; respect for the law has been greatly lessened; and crime has increased to a level never seen before."

Wall Street Crash

THE "ROARING TWENTIES" WERE A DECADE OF UNPRECEDENTED BOOM IN THE
UNITED STATES. AMERICANS BELIEVED GOOD TIMES WERE HERE TO STAY, BUT THAT
ALL CHANGED ON OCTOBER 24, 1929, WHEN THE STOCK MARKET, BASED ON WALL
STREET IN NEW YORK, STARTED TO FALL RAPIDLY.

As panic set in among investors, the crash became the worst in U.S. history and it would not fully recover from its effects for many years. At the end of World War I, the U.S. entered an era of extraordinary optimism and confidence. It turned its back on the problems of the world and concentrated its attentions at home. Recent inventions, such as the airplane and the radio, pointed to a bright new world where anything was possible. Women had new freedoms. Jazz, the movies, and speakeasies boomed, despite Prohibition. It seemed as if everyone was having a good time.

BOOM TIMES

Mirroring this optimism was an economic boom. At the start of the decade, Florida had experienced a land rush when speculation, fueled by easy-to-obtain credit, pushed up prices in this supposed semitropical paradise. However, a series of events, including a rail traffic embargo in October 1925, the Miami hurricane of 1926, and the realization by many speculators that they had been duped into buying worthless swampland, condemned the Florida land rush to history.

While a few observers saw the events in Florida as a warning, many Americans regarded it as a blip. Manufacturing continued to rise and every sector grew strongly. This, in turn, was reflected in the New York Stock Exchange.

SPECULATION EXPANSION

At the start of the century, the stock market had been restricted to professional investors. During the 1920s, ordinary Americans entered it, investing their savings in the hope of getting rich quick. Soon stock portfolios were a standard topic of conversation in barbershops and bars. As confidence grew, chauffeurs, maids, and teachers rushed to invest in the markets.

Bankers and brokers encouraged them to buy stock without cash, lending money to buy the stock, which they would pay back when the value of the stock rose (this practice, known as buying on margin, worked only while the market was rising). By August 1929, brokers had lent small investors more than $8.5 billion and some 25 million Americans had invested in the stock market. In the words of Yale economics professor Irving Fisher, "Stock prices have reached what looks like a permanently high plateau."

In fact, for those willing to see them, the warning signs of a stock-market problem had been gathering as early as 1928. Agricultural prices were falling and many of the Southern states were depressed with an economic outlook very different from the boom states of the North. House building was slowing and there was an overproduction in consumer goods, which piled up unsold in stores and warehouses. Steel production and car sales were also down, but few people paid attention while the stock market was still rising.

On March 25, 1929, a minicrash struck stock prices. The head of the Federal Reserve, Charles Mitchell, issued a statement after meeting with a group of bankers to discuss the markets. "We have an obligation to avert any crisis in the money market," he assured investors,

confirming that the banks would carry on lending money—for now. The market recovered, reaching its highest point on September 3, 1929, before beginning a roller coaster of highs and lows.

BLACK DAYS

On Thursday, October 24, 1929, the crash finally came. The stock market lost 11 percent of its value as panic spread and investors rushed to sell their stocks. Margins were called in and the ticker tape that recorded stock fluctuations could no longer keep up with the tumbling prices. Anxious crowds gathered at the New York Stock Exchange. The panic temporarily subsided that afternoon after a group of bankers put their own money into the market as a demonstration that it was still worth investing in, but 12.9 million shares were sold cheaply on "Black Thursday."

After a nervous weekend, the market plummeted again on "Black Monday," October 28, as investors continued their stampede out of the market. The market lost a further 13 percent of its value, and another 12 percent the next day, when 16 million shares were traded. Wealthy investors, such as the Rockefeller family, tried to calm the market by buying stocks, but this time the strategy failed. People rushed to the banks to withdraw their money. The stock market had lost some

$30 billion in just two days. After those tumultuous days, the market rallied slightly to reach a new peak on April 17, 1930. Then a longer slide took hold between April 1931 and July 8, 1932, when the market closed at its lowest level of the 20th century. By then, the stock market had lost 89 percent of its peak value. It would not reach the same value as September 3, 1929, until November 1954.

THE PRESIDENT PAYS THE PRICE

The dramatic falls in the stock market led to a massive loss of confidence in the financial system. Americans stopped buying goods and unemployment shot up. Herbert Hoover, who had become president earlier in 1929, thought that people were overreacting to the crash. He initially offered no federal help, assuming that the market would self-correct, and only belatedly began cutting taxes and increasing public works to inject money into the economy. But, by then, millions of Americans were out of work. Hoover's federal aid to the banks also arrived too late as the economy started to collapse. Protectionist measures intended to protect U.S. business from foreign imports had the effect of stifling international trade,

exporting the effects of the Depression around the world. In the election of 1932, President Hoover paid the price—probably

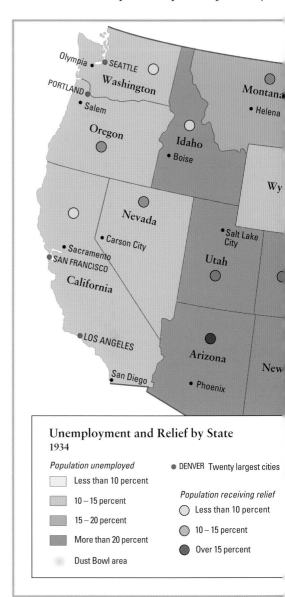

Unemployment and Relief by State
1934

Population unemployed

- Less than 10 percent
- 10 – 15 percent
- 15 – 20 percent
- More than 20 percent
- Dust Bowl area

● DENVER Twenty largest cities

Population receiving relief

- ○ Less than 10 percent
- 10 – 15 percent
- Over 15 percent

Every state in the Union was affected by the Stock Market Crash of 1929, plunging the country into the Great Depression, made worse by the droughts and crop failures across the Midwest in the early 1930s.

unfairly—for the financial collapse. The responsibility of dealing with the coming Depression would fall to a new president Franklin Delano Roosevelt and his New Deal. The recovery was helped enormously by the outbreak of war in Europe.

Munich Conference

DESPITE GERMAN EXPANSION IN THE 1930S, EUROPE'S POLITICIANS WERE SO RELUCTANT TO TACKLE HITLER THAT THEY GAVE IN TO HIS DEMANDS, A POLICY KNOWN AS APPEASEMENT. THIS POLITICAL WEAKNESS ENCOURAGED HITLER TO BELIEVE HE COULD ACT WITH IMPUNITY.

The first outside broadcast in TV history came from Heston Aerodrome in London on September 30, 1938. British Prime Minister Neville Chamberlain flew back from Munich, where he had held talks with German chancellor Adolf Hitler, dictator of Italy Benito Mussolini, and prime minister of France Édouard Daladier. Chamberlain announced: "The settlement of the Czechoslovakian problem, which has now been found is, in my view, only the prelude to a larger settlement in which all Europe may find peace."

Later, in Downing Street, he said, "This is the second time in our history that there has come back from Germany to Downing Street peace with honor. I believe it is peace for our time." Less than a year later, Europe was at war. Ever since, Chamberlain has been blamed for the disastrous handling of Adolf Hitler's territorial ambitions by Europe's democratic powers. He himself had said of Hitler, "I got the impression that here was a man who could be relied on."

HITLER'S RISE

Hitler had come to power as chancellor in 1933. He had risen to popularity by railing against the Treaty of Versailles, which imposed huge fines on Germany at the end of World War I, restricted the size of its army, and demilitarized the Rhineland next to the French border. Many Germans believed the agreement at Versailles was unjust and humiliating. In the political maelstrom that followed the defeat of 1918, the former soldier Hitler took over the small Nationalist Socialist German Workers' Party, or Nazis. Hitler appealed to the German public with his charismatic rhetoric, his promise to overturn the Treaty of Versailles, and his scapegoating of the Jews, liberals, and democracy for Europe's economic problems.

As chancellor, Hitler set about creating the "One Thousand Year Reich." He began testing the Allies by pushing claims to what he termed "Greater Germany," which included ethnic Germans left outside Germany after Versailles.

ANSCHLUSS AND ANNEXATION

Throughout the 1930s, Hitler's policies became increasingly belligerent. In 1933, he took Germany out of the League of Nations, which had been set up to arbitrate international disputes. In 1934, the Nazis organized the murder of the Austrian chancellor. In 1935, they reformed the Luftwaffe, the German air force, and began rearming, contrary to international agreements. In March 1936, German troops remilitarized the Rhineland. In 1937, Hitler signed the Anti-Comintern Pact with Mussolini's Italy. And in March 1938, he brought about the Anschluss, the union of Germany and Austria, and proclaimed the Greater German Reich.

In spring 1938, Hitler began calling for Germans living in the Sudetenland region of Czechoslovakia to be returned to German rule. It was clear by now to Europe's leaders that Hitler was determined to expand Germany, backed by military rearmament. The other Europeans were desperate to avoid war. Not only did memories linger of World War I, but both France and Britain remained in a fragile economic position. They were also wary of the Soviet Union, when Stalin offered himself as a potential ally. What was more, many Europeans now considered the Versailles Treaty overly harsh.

Chamberlain was convinced that if Germany reclaimed the Sudetenland, that would be the end of Hitler's demands. Hitler, of course, had no such intention. Chamberlain visited Germany three times to discuss the situation. On the first visit, Hitler demanded the return of the Sudetenland, which Chamberlain promised to consider. A week or so later, Hitler suddenly demanded the annexation of the Sudetenland within five days; Chamberlain rejected the request. Much to the rest of Europe's alarm, both the French and Germans now began to mobilize.

It thus seemed like something of a triumph when Chamberlain visited Hitler to avert war, this time with Mussolini and Daladier, in Munich on September 29–30, 1938. The three nations most threatened by German eastward expansion, Czechoslovakia, Poland, and the Soviet Union, were not represented in the talks. A Czech delegation attended, but was made to wait in another room. This time Chamberlain accepted Hitler's demand and gave the waiting Czech delegates a brutal choice: accept the dismemberment of their country or face the consequences—a likely German invasion—on their own. It was a fait accompli.

IT'S WAR

Chamberlain flew back to London still unaware of the magnitude of his humiliation at Munich. (He was not alone. President Franklin D. Roosevelt sent him a telegram saying "Good man.") He believed the talks had shown Hitler that the Allies were ready to interfere if his demands were too great. In fact, Hitler came away convinced of the opposite: that farther aggression could bring farther expansion at no risk of war. On March 15, 1939, Hitler took over the whole of Czechoslovakia. The next target to the east was Poland, and Hitler's invasion on September 1, 1939, would finally push the Allies into war.

Ultimately, the Munich Agreement had come to nothing. As one historian described the two days in September 1938: "Under pressure from the ruthless, the clueless combined with the spineless to achieve the worthless."

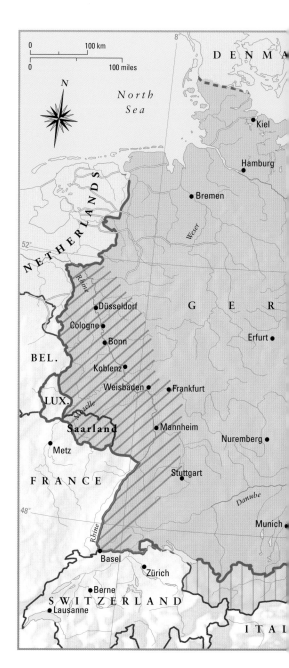

Hitler's expansion in Europe from 1936 to 1939 should have been warning enough for the other European leaders. His desire to overthrow the constraints of the Treaty of Versailles masked his more bloody ambitions.

Hitler's Annexations
1936–1939

Germany after 1919

Troops into demilitarized Rhineland March 1936

Anschluss (union with Austria), March 1938

Occupation of Sudetenland October 1938

Original Czechoslovakian border

Formerly Czechoslovakia occupied March 1939

Moravian and Slovak territory to Poland October 1938

Memel territory to Germany March 1939

Pearl Harbor

THE SURPRISE JAPANESE AIR ATTACK ON THE UNITED STATES' NAVAL BASE OF PEARL HARBOR IN HAWAII ON DECEMBER 7, 1941, WAS IN HINDSIGHT A MISTAKE FOR BOTH SIDES. FOR JAPAN, IT BEGAN A WAR THE COUNTRY SIMPLY COULD NOT WIN; FOR THE US, IT WAS NEARLY DEFEATED BEFORE IT BEGAN.

The origins of the attack on Pearl Harbor rest in Japanese ambitions to create what they called the Greater East Asian Co-Prosperity Sphere by driving out European colonial powers in Asia. In practice, the Sphere would be little more than a Japanese empire, intended to keep Japan supplied with resources that it lacked, particularly oil and coal.

Japan's war planners had decided that the only way their ambitions could succeed was through a preemptive strike to disable the major naval power in the Pacific, the United States. If the Japanese could destroy the U.S. Pacific Fleet, it would give them time to seize other territory, establish a perimeter around the Sphere and then negotiate with the U.S. for how much of it they would be allowed to retain.

SURPRISE ATTACK

The plan, devised by the commander of the Combined Fleet, Isoroku Yamamoto, was for a strike by 350 bombers, dive bombers, torpedo bombers, and fighter planes to be launched from aircraft carriers 230 miles (370 km) north of Hawaii. At 7:53 a.m. on December 7, the first wave of Japanese fighters and bombers descended on Pearl Harbor on the island of Ohau, where ships of the U.S. Pacific Fleet were moored close together with little defense. Personnel on the base were going about their Sunday morning routine. In less than two hours, five battleships were sunk or sinking, and another eight vessels damaged, while 320 airplanes had been destroyed or damaged. More than 2,300 Americans were dead and another 1,000 wounded. The raid had been a success.

But how had the Americans been taken so completely by surprise? For conspiracy theorists the answer is clear. Tensions with Japan had grown so great that the Americans must have known the attack was coming, but deliberately let it happen.

The finger of blame is pointed at President Franklin D. Roosevelt by those who believe that his support of the Allied cause meant that he was seeking a reason to take the country into World War I. In fact, the U.S. response to Japan's growing aggression reflected a combination of ignorance and blundering. It was not that Pearl Harbor's vulnerability had not occurred to them. Indeed, U.S. Pacific Fleet maneuvers in 1932 had focused on the scenario of a Japanese attack on the base. As early as January 1941, the Secretary of the Navy and the ambassador in Japan reported that any war was likely to begin with a surprise attack on Pearl Harbor. In November 1941, all U.S. Pacific bases, including Pearl Harbor, received warnings that hostile action was possible.

POOR U.S. DEFENSES

But the two men in charge at Pearl Harbor—General Walter Short and Admiral Husband Kimmel—took little action. Short was more concerned about treachery by the Japanese Americans living on Hawaii. He had all of his airplanes parked close together so they would be easier to protect from ground attack. Only four of his 31 antiaircraft batteries were even in place on December 7. Meanwhile Kimmel had no antitorpedo nets guarding his ships, and more than three-quarters of his 780 antiaircraft guns were unmanned. They had no program of aerial reconnaissance, although the island had 36 long-range planes for the purpose. And the island's eight new radar stations were in action for only a few hours each day.

Still, word of the coming attack could have reached Hawaii. Roosevelt had realized on December 6 that Japanese communiqués made war inevitable. U.S. Army Intelligence also realized that an attack on a U.S. base was imminent when it deciphered Japanese government messages to the Japanese ambassador in Washington, D.C., ordering him to deliver an ultimatum to the White House at precisely 1:00 p.m. on December 7, (7:00 a.m. in Hawaii), and then destroy his code machines. Intelligence reported their suspicions to Army Chief of Staff General George C. Marshall. However, it took two hours to find him and issue a warning to all U.S. bases. But the message to Hawaii was delayed. The War Department had to send it by commercial telegraph, because radio communications with the island were out of service. It arrived after the attack.

At 7:02 a.m. on December 7, a radar station in the north of Oahu detected inbound aircraft. The only officer on duty in the Army Operations Center was Kermit Tyler, a fighter pilot with no radar experience. He assumed the aircraft were B-17 bombers due to arrive from the mainland and told the radar operator, "Don't worry about it." The radar station shut down as scheduled.

But if the U.S. precautions against attack had been flawed, the attack did not achieve what the Japanese had hoped. Yamamoto was aware that the strike could only buy a short time in the Pacific. On the day of the attack, the carriers *Lexington* and *Enterprise* were at sea and survived. Pearl Harbor's refueling facilities, dry docks, and the base remained in use. When Roosevelt declared war on Japan on December 8, 1941, the resources the U.S. brought into the war made it clear that Japan's gamble had failed.

An overall view of Pearl Harbor and the effects of the Japanese attack on December 7, 1941.

Japanese Attack on Pearl Harbor
December 7, 1941

① Fifteen Kate high-level bombers from the *Akagi*, the first of 49 bombers to attack the four ships successively

② Kate torpedo bombers from the *Soryu*

③ Kate torpedo bombers from the *Hiryu*

④ Lead Kate torpedo bombers from the *Akagi* and *Kaga*

⑤ Follow-up Kate torpedo bombers from the *Soryu* and *Hiryu*

1. Tender *Whitney* and destroyers *Tucker, Conyngham, Reid, Case,* and *Selfridge*
2. Destroyer *Blue*
3. Light cruiser *Phoenix*
4. Destroyers *Aylwin, Farragut, Dale,* and *Monaghan*
5. Destroyers *Patterson, Ralph, Talbot,* and *Henley*
6. Tender *Dobbin* and destroyers *Worden, Hull, Dewey, Phelps,* and *MacDonough*
7. Hospital Ship *Solace*
8. Destroyer *Allen*
9. Destroyer *Chew*
10. Destroyer minesweepers *Gamble* and *Montgomery* and light minelayer *Ramsay*
11. Destroyer minesweepers *Trever, Breese, Zane, Perry* and *Wasmuth*
12. Repair vessel *Medusa*
13. Seaplane tender *Curtiss*
14. Light cruiser *Detroit*
15. Light cruiser *Raleigh*
16. Target battleship *Utah*
17. Seaplane tender *Tangier*
18. Battleship *Nevada*
19. Battleship *Arizona*
20. Repair vessel *Vestal*
21. Battleship *Tennessee*
22. Battleship *West Virginia*
23. Battleship *Maryland*
24. Battleship *Oklahoma*
25. Oiler *Neosho*
26. Battleship *California*
27. Seaplane tender *Avocet*
28. Destroyer *Shaw*
29. Destroyer *Downes*
30. Destroyer *Cassin*
31. Battleship *Pennsylvania*
32. Submarine *Cachalot*
33. Minelayer *Oglala*
34. Light cruiser *Helena*
35. Auxiliary vessel *Argonne*
36. Gunboat *Sacramento*
37. Destroyer *Jarvis*
38. Destroyer *Mugford*
39. Seaplane tender *Swan*
40. Repair vessel *Rigel*
41. Oiler *Ramapo*
42. Heavy cruiser *New Orleans*
43. Destroyer *Cummings* and light minelayers *Preble* and *Tracy*
44. Heavy cruiser *San Francisco*
45. Destroyer minesweeper *Grebe*, destroyer *Schley*, and light minelayers *Pruitt* and *Sicard*
46. Light cruiser *Honolulu*
47. Light cruiser *St Louis*
48. Destroyer *Bagley*
49. Submarines *Narwhal, Dolphin,* and *Tautog* and tenders *Thornton* and *Hulbert*
50. Submarine tender *Pelias*
51. Auxiliary vessel *Sumner*
52. Auxiliary vessel *Castor*

East Loch

Pearl City

Middle Loch

U.S. naval air station

Ford Island

Signal tower

Southeast Loch

Oil tanks

U.S. navy yard

Oil tanks

to open sea

N

0   50 metres

0   55 yards

Operation Barbarossa

Named after a German Holy Roman Emperor of the twelfth century, Operation Barbarossa, launched by Adolf Hitler on June 22, 1941, was the largest military invasion in history. Invading the Soviet Union promised much, but Hitler had overreached himself, sealing his own fate along with that of millions of German soldiers.

Since he had come to prominence in the 1920s, Adolf Hitler had wanted to expand Germany's borders to the east in search of *Lebensraum* ("living room") for the millions of ethnic Germans who dominated central Europe. He saw Slavs as subhuman people and viewed the Bolsheviks of the Soviet Union as little better.

THE MOLOTOV–RIBBENTROP PACT

In 1939, Hitler stunned the world by making a nonaggression pact with the Soviet dictator Joseph Stalin. In fact, the Molotov–Ribbentrop Pact was a logical step for both parties. Hitler wanted to avoid the possibility of war on two fronts, in the west against France and in the east against the Soviets. And Stalin wanted to buy as much time as possible to strengthen the Soviet defenses against the attack that would surely come. The pact included

secret terms by which Germany and the Soviet Union agreed to divide Poland between them. That duly happened after Germany's invasion of Poland in September 1939, which finally sparked World War II.

Having won lightning victories in much of continental Europe in 1939 and 1940, Hitler tore up the treaty. He sent 3.9 million Axis troops into the Soviet Union along a 1,800 mile (2,900 km) front, with the intention of conquering some of the richest land in Europe, including Ukraine, Belarus, and the oilfields of the Caucasus. The resources of these lands would then be channeled back to Germany and the inhabitants exported as forced labor, after which German settlers would move in and bring the territory under the control of Greater Germany.

To begin with, the invasion went well. The three German Army Groups—North,

Center, and South—made good progress on a front that stretched from the Baltic Sea to the Carpathian Mountains. But the Red Army facing them had perhaps 2.6 million men in the west, plus many more in the east, and it outnumbered the Germans in tanks by about four to one.

The German Army Group North used 600 Panzers to drive a wedge between the two Soviet armies facing it, but after a week Hitler ordered the Panzers to halt while the infantry caught up. This allowed the Soviets time to improve defenses around Leningrad. Army Group Center faced four Soviet armies, but by June 27, its Panzers were at Minsk, the capital of Belarus, about one-third of the way to Moscow. Army Group South faced determined resistance but still managed to reach Kiev, the capital of Ukraine.

Now, however, German commanders began to realize the strength of the enemy; every victory was bought at a high cost in casualties and in time. The Germans were running out of supplies but unable to range widely to find more. Yet the great prize of Moscow still looked to be within their grasp; they believed a rapid advance could capture the enemy capital.

OPERATION TYPHOON

The German generals were eager to seize their chance, but Hitler had other

The success of Russian resistance to Hitler was one of the deciding factors in the outcome of the war. This Soviet paper of 1945 reports on the conference at Yalta between Churchill, Stalin, and Roosevelt at the end of the war.

ideas. Halting the advance on Moscow, he sent Army Group Center's Panzers to more strategic targets: Leningrad in the north, and the Caucasus oilfield and the Donets Basin in the south. Then, growing impatient with the lack of progress, he brought the Panzers back from Leningrad to Army Group Center, and on October 2, launched Operation Typhoon, an assault on Moscow. By October 13, the lead Panzer divisions were within

90 miles (140 km) of their destination. But now the Germans had to halt to allow their supplies to catch up. Fall rain began to turn the unpaved roads to mud. At the same time, Stalin was able to form 11 new armies, some by moving troops from East Asia.

Now the operation had become a race against the winter. As the advance on Moscow continued, temperatures fell and the ground hardened. On December 2, German troops were 15 miles (24 km) from Moscow; they could see the towers of the Kremlin in the distance. But they could also see snow in the air. Winter had come. For any German general familiar with the defeat of Napoleon's *Grand Armée* by "General Winter" in 1812, when the French had been forced into a disastrous winter retreat from Moscow, their worst fears were about to come to pass, and history would repeat itself.

GERMAN FORCES COLLAPSE IN THE EAST
Once the snows came, the Wehrmacht was finished. It had virtually no winter gear. Its men died of exposure and their equipment broke down. A Soviet counteroffensive easily drove the Germans back 200 miles (320 km). Barbarossa had failed. Everywhere, determined Soviet resistance had far exceeded what Hitler had expected. At Leningrad, Moscow. and Kiev,

the Germans either failed to achieve their objectives or achieved them at such a cost that they were unsustainable.

The end of Barbarossa came in December 1941, but the war on the Eastern Front would carry on for nearly four years. Hitler would attempt new operations to win some advantage from the invasion—including Operation Blue in the Crimea, and the siege of Stalingrad—but these too failed. The eastern war cost more lives than any other military operation in history—by its end some 4.3 million Germans and 900,000 of their allies had died, together with around 8.7 million Soviet combatants and up to 20 million civilians. And in summer 1944, Operation Bagration began to push the Germans back out of Soviet territory. The Soviets would not stop pushing until April 1945, when the Hammer and Sickle flew over the Reichstag in Berlin.

German troop and tank movements during Operation Barbarossa from June 22 to early October, 1941, resulted in unprecedented loss of life, both of combatants and civilians.

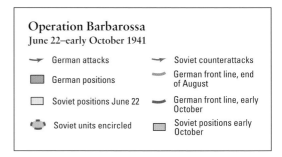

Operation Barbarossa
June 22–early October 1941

→ German attacks	→ Soviet counterattacks
▨ German positions	⌒ German front line, end of August
▢ Soviet positions June 22	▬ German front line, early October
⬮ Soviet units encircled	▨ Soviet positions early October

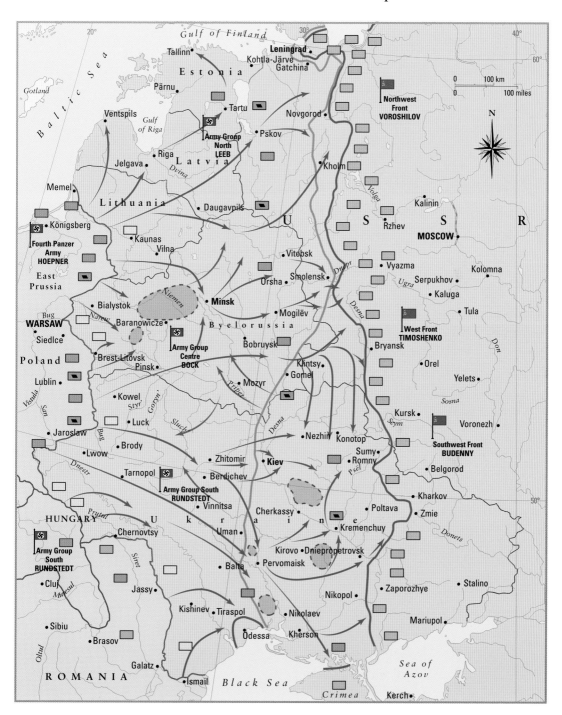

Dieppe Raid

BRITISH TROOPS LEFT MAINLAND EUROPE FROM DUNKIRK IN JUNE 1939. THEY DID NOT RETURN UNTIL D-DAY, JUNE 5, 1944, APART FROM ONE OCCASION IN AUGUST 1942. THE REASON THE DIEPPE RAID IS LARGELY OVERLOOKED TODAY IS THAT VIRTUALLY EVERYTHING THAT COULD GO WRONG WITH THE LANDING DID.

The raid seemed like a good idea at the time. For Britain's politicians, a raid on mainland France would have a number of advantages. It would provide a morale boost for the war-weary public after nearly three largely disappointing years of war and bad news. It would answer pleas from the Soviets for action that would take the pressure off the Eastern Front, where the Red Army was locked in an epic struggle with German forces. For military planners, such as Rear Admiral Louis Mountbatten, the Chief of Combined Operations, it would provide a rehearsal for the large-scale landing that would have to take place were the Allies to challenge Germany in Europe itself. Britain's Canadian allies, who were feeling aggrieved that their troops had seen so little action,

> *Rehearsals for the landing also went badly. The amount of air cover was reduced to avoid casualties among French civilians, and sea cover was also cut.*

actually lobbied to take part in order to help stimulate support and enthusiasm back home in Canada.

Dieppe had no particular strategic importance. It was just one of many German-held ports in France, but it was within range of the RAF's fighters and its name was also familiar enough that it was thought its temporary occupation would appeal to public opinion. The plan, devised by Mountbatten and his staff, was simple—too simple, in fact, in its complete lack of imagination. A landing force of 5,000 Canadians, 1,000 British commandos, and 50 U.S. Army Rangers would come ashore—there would be no preliminary bombardment to preserve secrecy—and destroy port facilities before it withdrew. A former burglar among the British commandos would break into

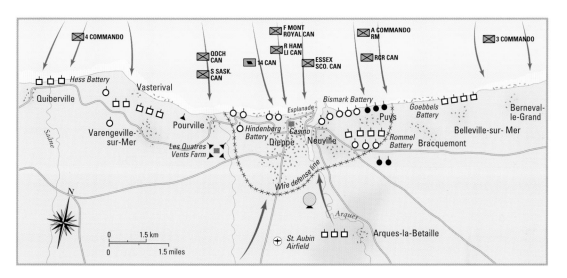

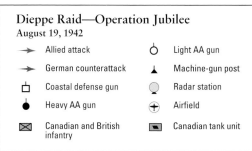

Dieppe Raid—Operation Jubilee
August 19, 1942

→	Allied attack	○	Light AA gun
→	German counterattack	▲	Machine-gun post
⊓	Coastal defense gun	◯	Radar station
●	Heavy AA gun	⊕	Airfield
⊠	Canadian and British infantry	◼	Canadian tank unit

The map shows the ill-fated and ill-conceived landings on Dieppe. It was supposed to provide a morale boost, but it proved to be both a military and a PR disaster for the Allies.

the dock offices to collect any documents that might be useful to military intelligence. A plan for British paratroopers to attack the German defenses on the headlands on each side of the town was abandoned because of poor weather.

The weather was not the only ominous sign. Rehearsals for the landing also went badly. The amount of air cover was reduced to avoid casualties among French civilians, and sea cover was also cut to avoid exposing battleships to coastal fire. The planners knew little about the beach or the defenses, and relied on vacation photos and aerial photographs. In addition, German agents had observed the troop buildup on the south coast and were aware that the British were paying a lot of attention to Dieppe. The port's defenders were, therefore, on high alert.

The delays continued past July 4, the original date for the operation. The assault finally began early on July 19, but it instantly lost the element of surprise when British vessels approaching the port exchanged fire with a small German convoy at 3:48 a.m. An hour later, at

4:50 a.m., Allied soldiers landed on mainland Europe for the first time in 38 months when British commandos and Canadians attacked artillery batteries on the flanks of the main landing area. The British were to the east at Berneval, but only 18 commandos were landed in the right place. Although they failed to capture the battery, they were able to keep the gunners distracted by sniper fire throughout the rest of the raid. In the west, more commandos captured the battery at Varengeville before withdrawing at 7:30 a.m. as planned; it was the operation's only clear success. Meanwhile, the Royal Canadian Regiment found its landing delayed by 20 minutes, so it attacked in daylight, without a smoke screen, against defenders put on alert by the exchange of gunfire at sea. The Canadians were quickly pinned down by German fire. Of 556 men, some 200 were killed and 246 captured. Another landing, by the South Saskatchewan Regiment, put most of the troops on the wrong side of a river, so few were able to reach their original objective.

Despite the failure of the initial landings, the main landing followed as planned a half hour later, as the Essex Scottish Infantry and the Royal Hamilton Light Infantry came ashore together with 27 Canadian tanks intended to provide cover for the infantry. In the event, many tanks had their tracks ripped off as they tried to find a purchase on the shingle beach, leaving them sitting ducks for the German gunners. The few that crossed the beach were blocked by concrete barriers. Meanwhile, the German machine-gun positions in the cliffs overlooking the beach—undetected in earlier reconnaissance photographs—raked the infantry with crossfire.

MISSION ABANDONED

The Canadian commander, Major General John Hamilton Roberts, was on HMS *Calpe* offshore, with no way of knowing what was happening, and no view of the beach because of the smoke screen. Despite this, Roberts now sent his reserves into an already disastrous situation. The landing craft came under heavy fire as they approached the beach. The mission dissolved into chaos. At 11:00 a.m., it was abandoned and the troops began to withdraw. Three hours later, when the last men escaped the beaches, they left behind 3,367 Canadians dead, wounded,

> *Three hours later, when the last men escaped the beaches, they left behind 3,367 Canadian dead, wounded or prisoners, together with 275 British commandos.*

Gold Beach at Arromanche was one of the D-Day landing sites from which the Allied forces launched their offensive against the Germans. Unlike the Dieppe landings, D-Day would prove to be a decisive turning point for the Allies.

or prisoners, together with 275 British commandos. There were 550 dead from the Royal Navy. Against such figures, the Germans had lost only 591 soldiers.

Dieppe was not the only disastrous rehearsal for D-Day. In April 1944, U.S. troops practicing amphibious landings at Slapton Sands in Devon were attacked in their landing craft by a German E-boat patrol. Some 638 men died in the attacks. A further 308 men perished during the landing, when they came under friendly fire from HMS *Hawkins*, which was using live ammunition to shell the beach in an effort to replicate real landing conditions. A PR disaster as well as a tragedy for those involved, the incident was largely hushed up until after D-Day.

Contemporary World

Modern times have seen no letup in disasters and mistakes that have had enormous consequences. Human error continues to figure largely in the cause of many crises, while nature also plays a role in current disasters. From hurricanes and tsunamis, oil spills and space accidents, to financial crises and banking disasters, our lives continue to be affected by the vagaries of nature and of man.

Space Shuttle *Challenger*

ON JANUARY 28, 1986, SPACE SHUTTLE *CHALLENGER* BROKE UP IN A FIREBALL JUST 73 SECONDS AFTER LIFTOFF IN FRONT OF THOUSANDS OF HORRIFIED SPECTATORS ON THE GROUND, INCLUDING THE ASTRONAUTS' FAMILIES, AND MILLIONS MORE WATCHING LIVE ON TV. IT SOON BECAME APPARENT THAT THE DISASTER WAS ENTIRELY AVOIDABLE—AND HAD BEEN PREDICTED.

The space shuttle was the pride of the National Aeronautics and Space Administration (NASA). It had been introduced in 1982 as a reusable vehicle to take astronauts and cargo into space, and was later instrumental in creating the International Space Station (ISS). Four shuttles were operational in the mid-1980s (a fifth was added in the early 1990s), which between them had flown numerous successful missions. Space travel was becoming as close to routine as it was ever possible to be.

So routine, in fact, that for the first time *Challenger* had a civilian teacher among its seven crew. Christa McAuliffe had been selected from 11,000 applicants for a program that aimed to put an "ordinary"

Technical problems forced a further postponement until January 28. Now the main concern was the weather at Kennedy Space Center.

person in space. Children in classrooms all over the country had followed her year-long training. The plan was for her to perform experiments and teach science lessons in space aboard the shuttle, which would be broadcast live. McAuliffe's six colleagues— five men and another woman—were trained astronauts and scientists, but they also encapsulated U.S. society; they were a cross-section of races, backgrounds, and religions from all across the country.

TECHNICAL PROBLEMS AND POOR WEATHER

The *Challenger* launch had originally been scheduled for January 22, but the previous shuttle mission had been delayed, which had a knock-on effect. Technical problems forced a further postponement

The space shuttle Challenger *disaster had a profound effect on NASA's space program, and after a second disaster, the shuttle service was finally shelved by NASA in 2011 due to lack of funding.*

until January 28. Now the main concern was the weather at the Kennedy Space Center in Florida. It was unusually cold for January, 31°F (-1°C), which was close to the minimum temperature below which a launch could not take place.

High winds and icicles forming on the rocket boosters worried the NASA scientists. Engineers also had concerns over NASA's contractor Morton Thiokol, which was responsible for building and maintaining the shuttle's solid rocket boosters (SRBs), the two long tanks on either side of the craft's huge main tank. The SRBs held fuel to power the shuttle after the initial phase of takeoff. They were assembled from six sections, which were held together by three joints. Each joint depended on two so-called O rings—seals designed to keep different parts of the rocket-fuel mixture apart. The vital role of the O rings was evidenced in their designation as "Critically-1"—in other words, if they were to fail, the shuttle would be destroyed.

The design of the O rings had caused NASA scientists some concern since the 1970s. It was known that if they got too cold, they became brittle and would not seal tightly. The engineers at Thiokol were aware of the problem, but neither they nor the mission directors at NASA thought that both O rings would malfunction at the same time.

EXPLOSION IN THE SKIES

On the morning of January 28 in Florida, the countdown began. The bitter cold prompted a conference call between NASA managers at the Kennedy Space Center and those at the Marshall Space Flight Center, where the booster rockets were made. The Thiokol engineers argued for a postponement because of the O rings, but the NASA managers in Florida were concerned that another failure to launch would put the whole shuttle program in jeopardy. After some discussion, the launch was approved.

Conditions, however, had conspired to provide the worst possible conditions. In addition to the unusually cold temperatures, there were very strong cross winds. When the countdown began, gray smoke was already escaping from the right solid rocket booster. The wind shear was the strongest ever recorded during a shuttle launch. It shattered an oxide seal that had been used to temporarily reinforce the brittle O rings.

TRAGEDY UNFOLDS

A minute after liftoff, the Thiokol engineers relaxed and began to congratulate one another. At 73 seconds, Mission Control ordered the shuttle to "throttle up," at which point the whole craft disintegrated in a cloud of flame and white trails of smoke. Before an audience of millions, including the families of the crew members, *Challenger* fell from the sky in pieces. It was a tragedy for the families of the crew watching in horror and a profound disaster for the future of NASA's space program.

President Ronald Reagan ordered an immediate investigation into the shuttle disaster. It concluded that the accident was caused by a failure of the O rings sealing a joint on the right solid rocket booster. The Nobel-prize winning physicist Richard Feynman, one of the highest-profile members of the commission, was damning in his judgment of NASA's management, which he accused of having massively unrealistic expectations of the reliability of the shuttle program. On live TV, he proved how the O ring could become fatally brittle by simply plunging it into ice-cold water. He declared, "For a successful technology, reality must take precedence over public relations, for nature cannot be fooled."

LESSONS LEARNT?

NASA was slow to learn its lesson. The space program was temporarily suspended to investigate the causes of the crash, but when it resumed in September 1988, the same management structures were still in place. In 2003, a second shuttle and its crew were lost when *Columbia* broke up on reentry into the Earth's atmosphere, with the loss of all seven crew members. Insulation tiles had come loose from the shuttle's underside, so the craft overheated.

The main questions after the second shuttle disaster again concerned NASA's management. The underlying problem was identified as the organization's decision-making and risk-assessment processes. That problem was perhaps best encapsulated by the job of the "shuttle program manager." A single individual was expected both to achieve a safe, on-time launch and to keep the project within budget. Such conflicting priorities were a recipe for disaster.

After *Columbia*, the space shuttle program was once again put on hold, this time for two years while investigations took place. Although the program was eventually resumed with a number of successful missions, it was ultimately shelved for being too expensive. The last space shuttle mission took place in 2011.

FACT FILE
Space Shuttle *Challenger*

Date: January 28, 1986

Weather Conditions: 31°F (-1°C); very strong crosswinds

Cause: The wind shattered an oxide seal used to temporarily reinforce the brittle O rings. The O rings thus failed to seal a joint on the right solid rocket booster

Mistakes: NASA was aware of the poor weather conditions and the questionable design of the O rings, but the launch was still approved

Aftermath: NASA was slow to learn its lesson. In 2003, *Columbia* was lost. In the years that followed, the shuttle program was ultimately shelved

Alaska Oil Spill

DUBBED THE WORLD'S MOST EXPENSIVE DRUNK-DRIVING CASE WHEN THE CAPTAIN OF THE OIL TANKER *EXXON VALDEZ* RAN HIS SHIP AGROUND IN THE WATERS OF PRINCE WILLIAM SOUND, ALASKA. IT SPILLED 20 PERCENT OF ITS CARGO, WHICH CAME ASHORE ALONG 1,100 MILES (1,770 KM) OF PRISTINE ALASKAN COASTLINE.

The *Exxon Valdez* had left the Trans-Alaska Pipeline at Valdez, Alaska, bound for Los Angeles, California, with a load of 53 million gallons (200 million liters) of Prudhoe Bay crude oil. The vessel had been guided out of Valdez and through the treacherous Valdez Narrows by William Murphy, an expert pilot. His task complete, he left the ship in the command of Captain Joe Hazelwood.

Hazelwood ordered his subordinates to divert from the shipping lane through Prince William Sound because of icebergs. After issuing strict instructions that the tanker was to return to the shipping lane once the iceberg danger had passed, Hazelwood retired to his cabin, leaving Third Mate Gregory Cousins and Helmsman Robert Kagan in charge of the ship. It was later claimed that the captain was sleeping off the effects of heavy drinking. He strenuously denied the allegation, although the official investigation into the accident did find that alcohol had played a part in the accident.

For reasons that remain unclear, Hazelwood's junior officers did not return to the shipping lane. Instead, the third mate ran the ship aground on rocks. Eight of its 11 tanks were damaged. Over the next six hours, some 10.9 million gallons (41 million liters) of oil escaped from the stricken ship. Much of the oil drifted south and west, concentrating close to

Hazelwood's junior officers did not return to the shipping lane. Instead, the third mate ran the ship aground on the rocks. Eight of its 11 tanks were damaged.

Bligh Island. It remained relatively limited, however, until March 26, when a strong storm with gale-force winds began to spread the slick. Spring tidal fluctuations of up to 18 ft (5.5 m), higher than at any other time of year, dispersed the oil over an ever-growing area. By March 30, the oil covered an area 90 miles (145 km) long.

The spread of the Exxon Valdez *oil spill in 1989 was made worse by severe storms and high winds dispersing the oil over a large area.*

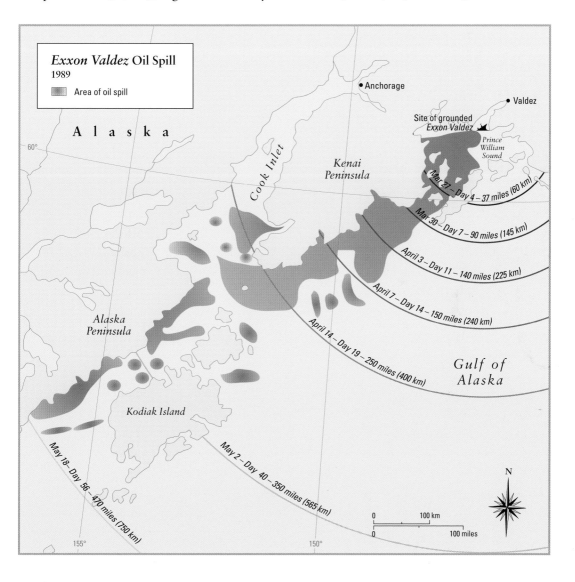

Eventually it spread 470 miles (756 km) from its point of origin. Along the pristine Alaskan coastline, the 200 miles (320 km) closest to the oil spill were particularly badly affected.

The oil caused an environmental disaster in the clean, fertile waters, with catastrophic effects on both marine and coastal life. At particular risk were some ten million seabirds, as well as sea otters, porpoises, sea lions, and whales. Almost 40,000 birds were killed as oil coated their feathers, preventing them from flying. The whole Alaskan commercial fishing industry was at risk as the delicate marine food chain was disturbed.

THE CLEANUP OPERATION

The biggest and most costly cleanup ever attempted to that point was put into place. It involved 11,000 people, 1,400 vessels, and 85 aircraft, cost more than $2 billion, and took two years. Three methods of cleaning the oil were tried: burning, mechanical cleaning, and chemical dispersants. None proved wholly successful. The rough weather made burning off the oil too difficult, and the thick oil clogged the booms and skimmers used for the mechanical cleaning. The dispersants were controversial and, when they did not work immediately, were discontinued. Instead, high-pressure washing with water was used on the coastline, although it destroyed the delicate microorganisms that lived on the rocks, further damaging the food chain.

SLOW RECOVERY

Two years into the cleanup, less than ten percent of the oil had been recovered. Much of the rest was absorbed into the sandy soil along the coast. Even today, Alaskan fishermen claim the ecosystem has not returned to its preaccident state. Shrimp and Dungeness crabs are only now slowly returning, and in 2010 the herring industry was still $400 million down on its 1989 business levels.

The Exxon oil company, which owned the tanker, admitted liability for the accident, and funded and carried out the cleanup. However, it engaged in years of legal wrangling to reduce the $5 billion punitive fine imposed on the corporation. In 2006, the amount was reduced to $2.5 billion on a federal appeal and the U.S/ Supreme Court cut it farther to $500 million in 2008.

LIABILITY

Exactly who was to blame for the *Exxon Valdez* disaster remains open to debate. The captain was asleep when the tanker ran aground, after reportedly having drunk five double vodkas, but it was actually the third mate who lost control of the ship. Exxon had apparently failed to install new radar systems or put sufficient crew on the tanker. And the U.S. Coast Guard had not inspected the *Valdez* due to its own staff reductions (after official reports into the disaster, the Oil Pollution Act of 1990 forced oil companies to build tankers with double hulls and better communications, and insisted that the Coast Guard enforce the regulations). But if the causes behind the accident are not clear, its victims certainly are—the wildlife along the coast of Alaska and the communities who depended on it are still feeling the effects of this devastating ecological disaster.

The cleanup operation after the spill took years and wrangling over responsibility cost billions of dollars.

Indian Ocean Tsunami

THERE WAS LITTLE WARNING FOR THE VACATIONERS ENJOYING THE SUN ON THE BEACHES OF THE INDIAN OCEAN ON DECEMBER 26, 2004. SOME MAY HAVE NOTICED THE ODD PHENOMENON OF THE WATER APPEARING TO RECEDE AWAY FROM THE BEACH, AND OTHERS MAY HAVE SPOTTED A WILDLY BOBBING BOAT OUT AT SEA.

Others still may have seen a smudge on the horizon, which soon became a wall of water, that overwhelmed the land. By the end of December 26, 227,000 people in 11 countries were either dead or missing after the most destructive tsunami ever recorded. Tsunamis are caused when earthquakes take place deep beneath the ocean. In this case, a massive earthquake measuring possibly as high as 9.2 on the Richter scale was triggered deep below the Indian Ocean. Its epicenter was at a depth of around 19 miles (30 km), and about 100 miles (160 km) north of Simeulue Island, off the coast of Sumatra, Indonesia. The initial quake—the third largest ever recorded—ruptured more than 600 miles (1,000 km) of sea floor, displacing it both horizontally and vertically, and jarring trillions of tons of rock with cataclysmic consequences.

By the end of December 26, over 227,000 people in eleven countries were either dead or missing after the most destructive tsunami ever recorded.

THE GROWING WAVES

Billions of gallons of water were sucked into the fissure and then expelled back out with great force. A series of waves emanated from the site of the rupture, up to 60 miles (100 km) long and as far as one hour apart. This "wave train" crossed the surface of the ocean as fast as a jetliner. Out in the open sea, the waves were only about 12 in (30 cm) tall and barely noticeable, but as they neared the shore and shallow water, the tops began traveling faster than the bottoms, causing the size of the waves to increase dramatically.

Waves tens of yards high hit the shore, releasing the equivalent energy of 23,000 Hiroshima-type atomic bombs and destroying everything in their path. Buildings were reduced to rubble in seconds, cars flipped over like toys, and some of the islands in the Maldives archipelago were completely submerged. The worst hit area was Aceh on the northern tip of Sumatra, the town closest to the epicenter of the earthquake, which

The 2004 tsunami around the Indian Ocean affected an extensive area and caused the deaths of over 227,000 people.

was almost completely obliterated. In Indonesia alone, an estimated 170,000 people died, one third of whom were children too small to stand up to the force of the water. However, few animal carcasses were found after the waters receded. Scientists believe this may have been because animals could feel the tremors

deep under the earth and instinctively fled to higher ground before the tsunami actually hit the shorelines.

AN OCEAN-WIDE DISASTER

The disaster struck countries around the Indian Ocean, including Sri Lanka, India, Malaysia, Thailand, Myanmar, the Maldives, and even Somalia on the east coast of Africa, killing hundreds of thousands of local people as well as many foreign vacationers. Many used cameras or cell phones to capture the approaching waves and the panic of people scrambling to safety in high buildings.

Amid the devastation, there were stories of extraordinary escapes. Some people recognized the signs that a tsunami was approaching, particularly the dramatic receding of the water to expose large stretches of sea floor. In Thailand, many people died when they went to the beach to see this strange phenomenon. However, on the island of Phuket, a ten-year-old British vacationer who had recently studied tsunamis at school was able to warn a whole beach of people to head to higher ground. In a similar scenario on the east coast of India, a villager saved his neighbors because he had seen a *National Geographic* television program about tsunamis and was able to warn them in time for them to seek higher ground.

FACT FILE
Indian Ocean Tsunami

Date: December 26, 2004

Countries Affected: Sri Lanka, India, Malaysia, Thailand, Myanmar, the Maldives, Somalia

Cause: Earthquake, possibly as high as 9.2 on the Richter scale

Epicenter: Located at a depth of around 19 miles (30 km), 100 miles (160 km) north of Simeulue Island

Statistical Data: The waves were up to 60 miles (100 km) long and came as far as one hour apart. They released the equivalent energy of 23,000 Hiroshima-type atomic bombs

Aftermath: Waterborne diseases; food and water shortages; whole communities left homeless; livelihoods destroyed; thousands of children orphaned. Restoration took many years, and still continues in places. Since 2004, a tsunami warning system has been in place across the Indian Ocean

The volume and velocity of the tsunami swept all before it, tossing cars around like toys, and destroying roads, buildings, and other infrastructure. The number of people who lost their lives was a staggering 227,000, with Indonesia suffering 170,000 casualties.

FROM DEVASTATION TO DISEASE

After the waters receded, contamination became a huge issue as rotting corpses and waterborne diseases spread. A lack of clean water and food was a major issue in many countries and sparked a humanitarian disaster in the hardest hit areas. Whole communities were left homeless, livelihoods were destroyed, and families were devastated, with many thousands of children left as orphans. The rebuilding effort took many years, and in many places it is still underway.

Since the 2004 disaster, a tsunami warning system has been introduced across the Indian Ocean. It detects seismic activity in the ocean and will hopefully relay a warning to all the relevant countries to give them time to evacuate coastal populations. In 2011, Japan suffered a devastating tsunami, so perhaps lessons still need to be learnt.

Dot.Com Crash

THE COMING OF THE INTERNET PROMISED CHANGES IN WESTERN CULTURE SIMILAR IN SCALE TO THOSE THAT FOLLOWED THE INVENTION OF MOVABLE TYPE IN THE 15TH CENTURY OR THE INDUSTRIAL REVOLUTION OF THE LATE 18TH CENTURY. A NEW BREED OF INTERNET ENTREPRENEURS SAW HUGE POTENTIAL IN THE EMERGING TECHNOLOGY, BUT THE PROMISED RETURNS WERE TOO GOOD TO BE TRUE.

It was only in 1990 that Tim Berners Lee invented what would become the World Wide Web and only in 1993 that the first browser for the Web, called Mosaic, was produced. Almost at once, however, entrepreneurs began to see the advantages of the new technology: it provided a market in which it was possible to reach people throughout the world, selling to them without the need for stores or staff in prime locations. All kinds of things could be sold: food, books, clothing, cars, even houses. Not only that, the Web made it possible to sell things that were not usually seen as tradable commodities, such as unsold vacations, airline seats, or hotel beds.

They convinced the money men, venture capitalists as well as regular investors ... that the Web offered untold wealth. And for a few individuals, it did ...

A YOUTHFUL REVOLUTION

In the second half of the 1990s, as Web-related technology grew rapidly and more and more households possessed new-generation browsers that made accessing the Web as simple as using the telephone, a whole new sector of companies emerged to take advantage. Some were electronic versions of already existing companies, mainly retailers, but what characterized the boom was a new generation of companies founded by strong-minded, savvy, highly convincing—and often very young—entrepreneurs. They convinced the money men, venture capitalists as well as regular investors who bought issues of stock, that the Web offered untold wealth. For a few individuals, it did. Among them were Martha Lane Fox, who made £13 million when she sold LastMinute.com, the company she cofounded; or Stephan Paternot, who raised $200 million for theGlobe.com, an early social networking site. Money poured into the "dot.com" sector. Stock prices of Internet start-ups went through the roof. The only problem was that no one had worked out viable business models for companies that often had nothing yet to sell and no public profile, but had huge start-up costs in terms of hardware, personnel (computer programmers were in short supply and could command high fees for their skills), and publicity.

Investors piled into the dot.com sector, often investing in businesses they knew nothing about. Stock prices went through the roof and disaster followed.

With so many new companies competing for the business of a growing but still small sector of the population, it took time—and money—to raise a corporate profile. Ironically, in the age of the new media, it seemed that the best way to raise that profile was through the traditional —and expensive—media: newspaper ads and, above all, TV commercials. Web companies were helped, however, by the historically low interest rates of the mid-1990s, which meant that money could be raised cheaply from banks. No one wanted to be left out. Investors threw money at ideas they weren't even sure they understood. NASDAQ, the U.S.-based index of stock market prices for technology-based companies, saw rapid growth in 1999 and 2000, doubling its value in just a year.

Investors threw money at ideas they weren't sure they understood ... stock-market prices for technology-based companies saw rapid growth in 1999 and 2000.

THE RACE AGAINST FAILURE

However, in many cases no one was actually producing anything. No service was being sold or delivered that could raise money. The pattern in which the dot.coms came to work went like this: get as much money as possible for a start-up and then spend it all in a race to make the brand strong enough to survive before the money ran out. Once the money went, that was it. Some companies had business models that allowed them to play a long game; Amazon and Google were two of the biggest players, but neither of them made a profit for years. Many more firms burnt out without having ever covered their costs. Some had over-estimated the demand for their products. Others were based on technological developments that simply never happened, such as high-speed fiber-optic cables that would not become common for another decade or so. A few firms, such as the ISP Worldcom, were tempted into illegal accounting to try to stave off their inevitable decline.

There were other factors behind the fall of the market. The U.S. courts ruled that Microsoft, the most wealthy of all the new technology companies, was a monopoly and would have to be broken up into parts. America Online (AOL) fell victim to an unwise merger with Time-Warner and lost its leading position in the market. At the start of 2000, a slowdown in the global economy also led to rising interest rates, which made money more expensive to service. In a new climate of realism, investors and journalists began to take a closer look at the track record of many Web companies and became increasingly concerned that they showed no signs of making a profit any time soon.

THE BUBBLE BURSTS

By the end of 2000, the bubble had burst. Within months, dot.coms were closing everywhere, even some of the biggest. Freeinternet.com had become the fifth biggest Internet service provider in the U.S., with 3.2 million users, but could not afford the $19 million it had spent to attract them—given that its subscriptions had actually raised only $1 million. Boo.com had the idea for an online fashion store years before the ultrasuccessful net-a-porter.com, but found that throwing an average of $30 million a month at advertising drove it out of business after just six months.

The electronic marketplace survived, of course, but in a shape that more closely resembled the traditional marketplace. Players that were able to ride out the early roller coaster, such as Amazon and eBay, went on to discover that there were indeed fortunes to be made. But their business practices were tighter and more strictly controlled. The days when venture capitalists raced to invest in projects more from a fear of being left behind than from any realistic promise of returns were gone—for the time being.

Some dot.coms were based on developments that never happened, such as high-speed fiber optics that would not become common for another decade.

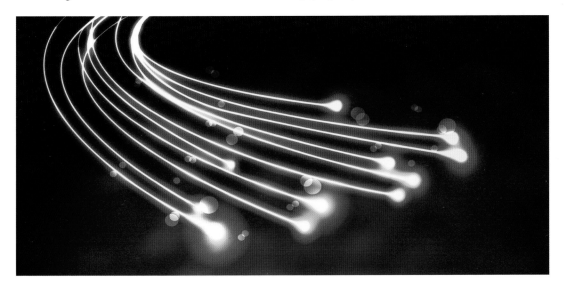

Hurricane Katrina

THE NORTH AMERICAN CONTINENT IS NO STRANGER TO HURRICANES, WHICH HAVE STRUCK WITH DEVASTATING REGULARITY THROUGHOUT THE 20TH CENTURY. THE 21ST CENTURY BEGAN FAIRLY QUIETLY UNTIL THE 2005 HURRICANE SEASON SAW THREE OF THE SIX MOST POWERFUL HURRICANES EVER MEASURED IN THE ATLANTIC MAKE LANDFALL ON THE GULF COAST.

Of the three major hurricanes in 2005, it was the weakest, Katrina, that did the most damage. When it crossed the Gulf of Mexico in August 2005, it was a category 5 hurricane—the strongest possible, with winds of up to 175 mph (280 km per hour)—but by the time it made landfall it had weakened to a category 3 or 4. However, when it struck land on August 29, 2005, it was still the largest tropical storm ever to hit the U.S.

Katrina tore into the Gulf Coast all the way from Florida to Texas, leaving about a million people homeless. Although many people had evacuated the region, the majority had not. At least 1,823 people died, with more than 705 unaccounted for. The hurricane's main impact fell on the states of Louisiana and Mississippi, with particularly severe devastation being visited on the historic city of New Orleans.

Water flooded into New Orleans, whose bowl-like shape prevented it from draining away. Water collected in the city's streets and buildings where it became stagnant.

Climatologists and emergency planners had long known that New Orleans was a disaster waiting to happen. The National Weather Service had warned that a hurricane there would cause "human suffering incredible by modern standards." The city had a population of some 485,000, but much of its area lay an average 6 ft (2 m) below sea level.

The path and velocity of Hurricane Katrina from its origins in the Caribbean, through the Gulf of Mexico, and across the eastern United States.

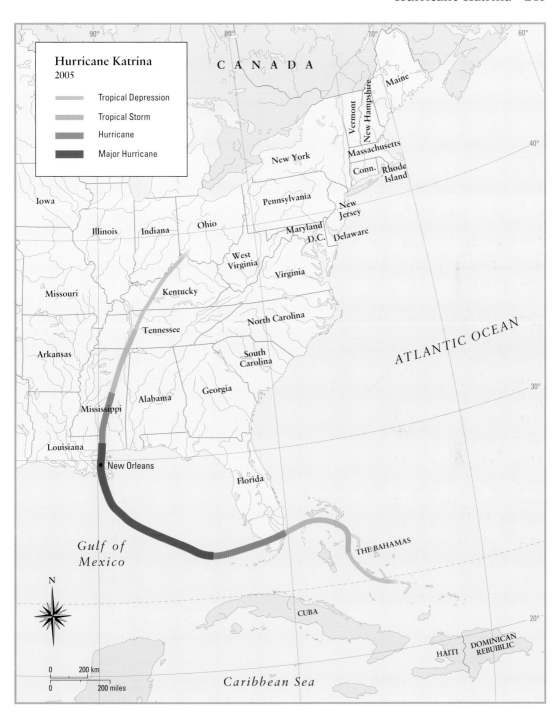

Hurricane Katrina
2005

Tropical Depression
Tropical Storm
Hurricane
Major Hurricane

Water surrounded the city on all sides: the Mississippi River, the Gulf of Mexico, and Lake Ponchartrain. The city was protected only by levees—thick earth embankments. These had been built from the late 19th century onward to withstand storms, but it was well known that they would be inadequate if a major hurricane or tidal surge struck. There was also some evidence that the levees had not been maintained.

When Hurricane Katrina hit, it brought a storm surge 28 ft (8.5 m) high that inundated communities along the Gulf coast in Mississippi and Louisiana, and opened dozens of holes in the levees, which were unable to withstand the volume of water. Water flooded into the city of New Orleans, whose bowl-like shape prevented it draining away. Water collected in the city's streets and buildings, where it became stagnant and disease-laden as corpses and sewage piled up.

By August 31, more than 80 percent of the city had been flooded. Some areas were under as much as 15 ft (4.6 m) of water. To make matters worse, although about a million citizens had left the city and surrounding area, about 100,000 people remained, many of whom were the most vulnerable in society, either elderly or poor. Now homeless, they were directed to the city's main sports arena, the Louisiana Superdome, itself damaged by the storm.

A HUMANITARIAN DISASTER

Television crews from around the world covered the unfolding humanitarian disaster as residents tried to escape the flooding. Many were filmed from helicopters as they waited desperately on their roofs for rescue. More than 20,000 refugees—many of them frail, sick, or old, and predominantly African-American— arrived at the Superdome, where conditions soon became unsanitary and swelteringly hot. At the city's convention center, which became a second shelter despite not having been designated as one, terrified evacuees were terrorized by roaming gangs. It was soon apparent that there was insufficient fresh water, food, and basic sanitary provision for the thousands left in the city. The situation was worsened by looting and general lawlessness.

A SLOW RESPONSE

The response to the disaster was inadequate at all levels of government. Although New Orleans had rehearsed a response to a hurricane only the year before, the city authorities had no effective transportation or crime prevention strategies in place. It could not get supplies in or evacuees out, and it could not prevent the looting. The federal response was equally inadequate. The Federal Emergency Management Agency (FEMA), which was supposed to

Hurricane Katrina caused a storm surge that broke through the levees and left destruction in its wake. These yachts have been tossed around like toys in a bath by the force of the storm and the waves, causing untold damage.

coordinate the response to such disasters, was slow to appreciate the scale of the catastrophe. President George W. Bush himself was also widely criticized for not appearing in the devastated region for four days, and then only visiting briefly and mainly flying overhead. Two thirds of the Americans polled felt that the president's response had been inadequate. In economic terms, Katrina would prove to be the worst hurricane in American history thus far. It cost an estimated $81 billion in property insurance claims, with 275,000 homes destroyed—up to ten times more than any other natural disaster in the United States. As many as 400,000 jobs were lost along the Gulf Coast, prompting an economic crisis whose effects lasted even longer than the physical damage. The rebuilding and reconstruction is still ongoing.

Banking Crisis

THE FINANCIAL CRASH THAT BEGAN IN 2008 TRIGGERED THE GREATEST GLOBAL ECONOMIC CRISIS SINCE THE GREAT DEPRESSION OF THE 1930S. BLACK-AND-WHITE PHOTOGRAPHS OF THE JOBLESS STANDING IN LINES AT SOUP KITCHENS WERE REPLACED BY NEW PICTURES OF TEARFUL BANK EMPLOYEES LEAVING THEIR JOBS, CARRYING THE CONTENTS OF THEIR DESKS IN CARDBOARD BOXES.

The crisis crept up on many people virtually unnoticed. Every country had its own iconic moments when the scale of the crisis became apparent. In Britain, it was the long lines of panicked customers descending on branches of the Northern Rock building society in September 2008, fearing for their savings, or the shocking news two months later of the bankruptcy of Woolworths, whose red store fronts had been familiar sights in almost every British town for decades.

In the United States, it was the collapse of the highly aggressive, ostensibly successful Lehman Brothers bank that same September—the largest bankruptcy in U.S. history—followed by the collapse of two government-supported enterprises, mortgage providers that were part of the fabric of everyday life for millions: Fannie Mae and Freddie Mac.

HOUSING BOOM

The causes of the collapse were varied, but most commentators agreed that the immediate trigger was a boom in the U.S. housing market, which peaked in 2007 but turned out to be built on sand. Competitive banks and financial institutions had fallen over themselves in their eagerness to lend money to people who would previously have been considered a risk of bad debt—so-called subprime mortgages. But with historically low interest rates, the banks

The problem can be traced back to the international deregulation of the financial markets in the early 1980s, which left the banks free to operate as they chose ...

were eager to take a risk in order to earn additional commission.

However, the roots of the problem can be traced farther back to the international deregulation of the financial markets in the early 1980s, which had left banks largely free to operate as they chose. Those regulations still in place applied mainly to the deposit or lending banks. But a whole sector had emerged that did much the same thing, but without the same level of regulation. These investment banks and other institutions were also eager to offer loans to homeowners, with their funds often derived from short-term loans that left them vulnerable. The banks spread their risks by creating new financial products to sell, parceling up subprime debt into bundles to sell to investors as so-called mortgage-backed securities and collateralized debt obligations, which were widely traded. Few people understood the intricacies of the system, but the lure of the U.S. housing boom was so great that investors from around the world rushed to part with their money. And the ready availability of credit cards and other easy credit encouraged a consumer boom.

BANKING BUST

When the U.S. housing bubble burst in 2008, foreclosures began to rise along with interest rates. By August 2008, 9.2 percent of U.S. mortgages were in default; a year later the figure was 14.4 per cent. Financial institutions that had invested in real estate—either directly or

Money changers in Tirana, Albania, wait for customers in an open air market. Albania descended into anarchy in 2009, following the collapse of the banking system in that country as part of the global crisis.

Investment bank Lehman Brothers went bankrupt in September 2008, causing shock waves throughout the global banking sector.

a third of the nation's wealth. None of the five survived intact: Goldman Sachs and Morgan Stanley became commercial banks, which meant they had to accept greater regulation, while Bear Stearns and Merrill Lynch were sold off at bargain prices. The US government had to inject money to keep these four afloat, but not for Lehman Brothers, which was allowed to go bust.

TOO BIG TO FAIL

Governments around the world faced similar problems. Banks had grown so large that their failure would bring ruin to thousands of small companies and millions of savers. More than a hundred mortgage lenders went bankrupt in 2007 and 2008. Although banks and other financial institutions were private businesses, governments felt obliged to support many of them through "bail outs" to prevent the economic crisis from worsening. The British government nationalized or part-nationalized a number of banks, including Northern Rock and the

indirectly—were suddenly exposed to huge losses. Banks that had leveraged all their money were now in no position to get their loans back. They ran short of cash. In 2008, the top five US investment banks reported debts of some $4.1 trillion, about

Royal Bank of Scotland, making taxpayers liable in part for these banks' bad debts. In Iceland, all three of the country's major banks collapsed in what was proportionally the largest financial collapse experienced by any nation.

On a larger scale, the crisis was spreading through the global economy. Many currencies began to suffer on the money markets, as investors moved to perceived stronger currencies, such as the U.S. dollar and the British pound. The value of the New York Stock Exchange fell by more than half in 17 months, a drop similar to that during the Wall Street Crash of 1929. Worse, the banking crisis and the loss of investor confidence led to a shortage of what the system needed most in order to survive: credit. No-one wanted to lend money.

About one third of the apparatus for lending money in the United States was not functioning. With less cash in circulation, businesses in many countries began to fail at a much quicker rate. As unemployment rose, so mortgage defaults increased around the world. The circumstances appeared right for a new global depression.

In Europe, governments followed suit, pumping money into circulation—a strategy known as "quantitative easing"—while adopting austerity measures...

GOVERNMENT REACTION

Some governments were quick to react. The U.S. government injected $700 billion into the economy in October 2008. In Europe, governments followed suit, pumping money into circulation—a strategy known as "quantitative easing" —while also adopting stringent austerity measures in order to reduce public spending. The political and social fallout were vast, with governments falling, international alliances shifting and violent unrest on the streets from protestors objecting to both "fat-cat" bankers and cuts to government spending and welfare.

The knock-on effects were felt particularly in the Euro zone. While the U.S. economy began to stabilize in 2009 and 2010, and even to grow slowly, the combination of the banking and credit crisis and the inherent weaknesses of the European single market threatened to drive "weaker" economies such as Greece, Spain, and Portugal out of the Euro altogether. The ramifications of this crisis will remain within the global economy for some time; and the outlook in the Euro zone is still uncertain, particularly for Greece as it attempts to stay afloat and within the Euro zone.

Index

Acknowledgments

We would like to thank the following for the use of their pictures reproduced in this book:

Corbis
143, 151, 155

Shutterstock
11, 21, 32, 42, 45, 50, 57, 62, 66, 69, 80, 83, 88, 92, 100, 104, 108, 111, 113, 126, 129, 130, 134, 138, 146, 164, 168, 187, 193, 197, 203, 207, 209, 211, 215, 217, 218

All other photographs and illustrations are the copyright of Quantum Publishing. While every effort has been made to credit contributors, the publisher would like to apologize should there have been any omissions or errors—and would be pleased to make the appropriate correction for future editions of the book.